# TEAMWORK:

## WE HAVE MET THE ENEMY AND THEY ARE US

PUBLISHED BY THE CENTER FOR MANAGEMENT
AND ORGANIZATION EFFECTIVENESS

CMOE

# ACKNOWLEDGEMENTS

A book on teamwork is the end product of a process that involves a team of people. We are responsible for what ends up on the printed page, but would have been unable to develop and articulate these ideas without the insights, criticism, and encouragement of many people. Our colleague, Chris Johnson contributed to Chapter 8 and was of great help in the production process.

Our deepest appreciation goes to the hundreds of executives and managers who have participated in our TeamExcel programs. Their reactions and thoughtful comments have been invaluable. They were willing to provide us the opportunity to try new ideas and to see teams struggling to excel.

Dr. Roy Yamahero, retired Vice President of Human Resources, Federal Express, encouraged us to experiment and learn from the outdoors. He has been a great source of inspiration. Walter Kimbrough, Director, Federal Express Leadership Institute, has provided rich opportunities to learn from consulting projects with teams and kept us around long enough to learn from our mistakes.

The team at Ebert Architect, Inc.: Derry Ebert, Betty Mead, and Kristi Robbins provided support, helpful comments, and a quiet place to write. Helen Hodgson's editorial inputs immensely improved the final product.

Lastly, we are each members of a family team. Their support, encouragement, and patience during this project constitute a tribute to what good teamwork is all about.

# TEAMWORK:

## WE HAVE MET THE ENEMY AND THEY ARE US

Matt M.
Starcevich, Ph.D.

Steven J.
Stowell, Ph.D.

**The Center For Management and Organization Effectiveness**

245 S.E. Madison Blvd.
Bartlesville, Oklahoma 74006
(918) 333-6609

9146 South 700 East
Sandy, Utah 84070
(801) 569-3444

CMOE PRESENTS

THE SECOND IN A SERIES ON

# PARTNERSHIPS IN THE WORK PLACE

## THE CENTER FOR MANAGEMENT AND ORGANIZATION EFFECTIVENESS (CMOE)

Organized in 1979 with the following mission:

1. To provide training for managers and employees.
2. To solve difficult organization problems.
3. To design and implement quality human resource systems.
4. To conduct practical and useful organization research.
5. To publish the results of our work.

Our staff all hold advanced degrees in the behavioral sciences and are consulting with many of the Fortune 500 firms to improve management and organization effectiveness.

# TABLE OF CONTENTS

# FOREWARD

The human resource development profession is striving to meet a critical need: to train people to be good managers and leaders. Needless to say, we are struggling. For that matter we can't even agree that being a good manager is the same as being a good leader. Some writers have told us that a manager is a manager and that a good leader is a distinctly different breed of cat. Other writers have taken the position that a good manager always shows the traits of a good leader. It seems abundantly clear that we don't have a very good idea of what it takes to be a good manager/leader or, even if they are one and the same.

For the past twenty-five years I have gravitated towards the position that a good manager is a good leader. Being skilled at both requires learning to process the behavior of a team: to clarify the teams objectives, focus their efforts and maximize cooperative teamwork. The dilemma we face is how to teach the skills of processing behavior. When we observe good managers and leaders, they have several distinctive characteristics in common:

> They perceive their work group as a team that depends upon cooperation among its members.
> They listen intently to their team members.
> They are sensitive to their team members' needs and actively encourage each members' participation.

I believe that the most effective way of teaching the processing skills that these leaders display is by the experiential method: The participant experiences firsthand the processing of others' behavior, observes the results, evaluate the successes and the failures, and determines the effectiveness of his/her own behavior. This book describes that process.

This is an excellent resource for the novice as well as the more experienced manager/leader. Teams are observed in action along with the keys to the process that leads to improved teamwork. A "how-to" book on the skills that are needed to improve teamwork has been lacking, and this book by Starcevich and Stowell fills that gap. What I like most is being there with a team as the members struggle to meet various outdoor challenges. The issues that emerge through the group process, issues that stand in the way of task accomplishment, are reminiscent of what I have seen in too many teams. This book can help you better define and manage these issues through an understanding of the skills needed to process the behavior of a team.

Having facilitated groups striving toward genuine teamwork, I find the important issues for peak performing teams concisely, accurately, and interestingly presented in this valuable reference book. It is a must book for your training library and for the line manager's/leader's bookshelf.

Roy S. Yamahiro, Ph.D.
Retired Vice President
Human Resources
Federal Express Corp.

# 1
# WHY TEAMWORK?

"When teamwork kicks in, nobody can beat you."
–Don Shula, Head Coach, Miami Dolphins
...Only NFL team to attain a perfect 17-0 season

During the decade when the NFL has established parity through giving winning teams the toughest schedules and the lowest draft picks, Bill Walsh has found a way to beat the system. The San Francisco 49'ers have been to the play-offs six consecutive years and have won three Super Bowl titles during the 1980's, a feat no other team can claim.

How do teams like the Dolphins and the 49'ers achieve these records–better athletes? San Francisco drafted wide receiver, Jerry Rice, the 1989 Super Bowl's Most Valuable Player, after 15 other teams passed on him. At the same time, parity has humbled such coaching pillars as the Pittsburgh Steelers' Chuck Noll and Dallas Cowboys' Tom Landry. We submit that, in the NFL, the technical side of coaching and computerized scouting of college football players are constants; the key is how and if the coach can develop cohesive teamwork among a group of individual superstars.

Outside of sports, is teamwork important? How many times have you heard successful managers say, "The department exceeded its sales goals, improved customer satisfaction, decreased costs, and increased operating efficiency–all because of me. I alone deserve all the credit"? Or, "If it weren't for me, I would never have been here and able to say 'One small step for man, one giant step for mankind'"? Give us a break!

## WHY A BOOK ON TEAMWORK?

Whether it's two people, a department, or an organization, teams are the means by which great things get done. Unfortunately, not all work groups exhibit teamwork. The difference is the subject of this book. How do groups develop that sense of community and cohesiveness, or what is Don Shula's secret? When and how does teamwork kick in?

The press and our own consulting experience point to the need for American managers to be both willing and able to build and maintain high performing teams. One key to regaining our competitiveness will be how successful managers are in creating the climate for teamwork to grow and develop–the Japanese have shown this to be true.

We believe it doesn't just happen by accident. Teams work at building spirit and commitment; they talk about how they are doing, and they are willing to invest time and money to protect and enhance the basic team fabric and integrity. In a team, people care about each other and are concerned about how their actions and attitudes affect each other.

Managers report they spend from fifty to ninety percent of their time in group activity, yet they seem to concentrate their efforts on managing individuals. Most managers have little or no knowledge of group dynamics.

In this book you will discover the inner dimensions and facets of how groups become teams and how group dynamics can be managed. Observing groups at work adds clarity to the very subtle and often subliminal concept of teamwork. It is not magic and there is no secret; it can be explained and put into practice by every manager.

We will be examining the phenomenon of teamwork in a unique environment, the outdoors. By placing groups of people in an outdoor setting, we have been able to create a level playing field on which the presence or absence of teamwork, not the technical or individual makeup of the group, has become the determining factor for success.

In the outdoors, the groups vividly see those processes that allow teamwork to express itself and thrive, with fruitful results, or to wither and die on the vine. The activities reported here are a vehicle that allows participants and you to observe and unmask the common enemies of teamwork and to see more clearly the obstacles that all too frequently are created within the team.

Team afflictions are widespread: destructive and over-charged competitiveness, individualism, over-inflated egos, personal greed, and technology such as computers that drive us into ourselves and have the potential of isolating us so we can "do our own thing." Seeing the impact of these afflictions on the quality of teamwork is the first step towards a more effective team.

## WHO SHOULD READ THIS BOOK?

We welcome you to this journey into the outdoors where you will have some fun but, more importantly, learn how to build and maintain effective teamwork. For those of you who believe the West was won by rugged individualism, we can't argue. However, leading out and individualism are only two of the many roles that need to be played on an effective team. Although individualism may play a part, exceptional accomplishments–more often than not–require a group of people with collective courage and effort.

We will define, illustrate, and provide a fun and interesting way to look at the phenomenon of teamwork from multiple perspectives: The team members, third-party observers, trainers, and senior executives who have the years of experience and training necessary to offer sage advice to those of us who are still struggling to define teamwork.

We believe this book is particularly relevant to the following people:

- Managers and executives, particularly those faced with creating a new team or changing the way their existing team operates and solves problems.

- Personnel and human resource people who are asked, as trusted allies, to consult with managers on improving teamwork.

- Trainers who are interested in using the outdoor laboratory and experiential learning as a dynamic method of empowering participants to change and grow.

## OVERVIEW OF THE CONTENTS

Teamwork is a process that can be experienced outdoors as well as in the work place. And lessons learned in one environment can be applied equally well in another. This book describes actual teams that have participated in a variety of outdoor team-building programs. The programs have been as long as five days and as short as one. Each account has been chosen as illustrative of one of the phases all teams go through in the progression from inception of the team to fully functioning interdependence. A sampling of teams has been selected because, for a particular event, one or another best illustrates why some teams work together better than others. Not all teams engage in the events reported here, nor are these events an exhaustive report of all the team-based activities that could be used to improve teamwork.

The majority of the accounts describe teams that have failed to succeed at their assigned task. We focus on failure to highlight those factors that contributed to each team's demise, not to suggest that all teams are failures. The best team discussions and insights have resulted when teams have had to explain why they failed.

The client teams we work with already see themselves as effective. What they are seeking from us is to improve on their effectiveness–to be stretched and tested and to grow as a group. Not all teams fail, but these accounts are typical of how the majority of teams approach the outdoor challenges they face. As with the actual teams, if you focus on success or failure, you will miss the important opportunity to explore how the teams functioned in performing the tasks: their processes.

Each account has been written as an independent narrative followed by a summary of the key points that would have contributed to better teamwork. The summaries are in varied formats including a didactic approach, a panel-of-experts' discussion, participants' personal reflections, a fable, and the team's own reflective discussion.

Our hope is that you can translate the outdoor metaphors and summaries to the work place and to situations within your own teams. The crucial leap involves taking the lessons these teams have learned experientially and applying the concepts to improving your teamwork.

Like any journey, many routes can be taken. You don't have to read the book from cover to cover to capture the significant messages. Choose those topics or aspects of teamwork of most interest and zero in on them. We hope the format will lend itself to an enjoyable journey into the inner workings of group dynamics and teamwork.

Chapter 2 and 3 discuss the problems that start-up teams face. Issues of individuality versus team play, low trust, who's in and who's out, and an unwillingness to listen will be explored.

Chapter 4 and 5 study the issues existing groups have in working as a team to solve problems and accomplish their tasks. Specific ways to overcome poor planning, lack of commitment, unequal participation, an inability to deal with differences in the group, and the under-utilization of resources are presented.

In Chapter 6 and 7 we look at the problems two independent teams have when they must operate and cooperate as one. Managers who confront the challenge of melding two competing groups into a team will find this section of particular value.

The subject of teamwork would be incomplete without a discussion of resistance to change. Chapter 8 and 9 explore why teams become comfortable and resist change even in the face of extinction. Our focus is on not only why this happens, but what teams can do to overcome this growing entropy.

Successful teamwork is the subject of Chapter 10 and 11. Here readers can watch a group of individuals operate as a winning team. Through this unique looking glass, readers see first hand the components of effective teamwork and how team members create and maintain the elements necessary for team survival.

Chapter 12 is for the reader who is concerned with bringing team members to a common vision and way of operating. We discuss the importance of a team vision, consider what this vision entails, and suggest a process any manager can implement with his/her team to establish the commitment needed to adopt a vision of team excellence.

For those teams or managers who would like to start off by assessing their team's strengths and weakness, Appendix I is the answer. We present a model for thinking about team effectiveness and a questionnaire to assess how your team rates itself on each component of this model.

Appendix II is provided for readers interested in using outdoor adventure-based training to empower their teams. Specific guidelines, as well as caveats, are presented. In Appendix III we present unique issues when facilitating an outdoor adventure-based team-building exercise.

# 2

# A New Team Heads For Shark Island

It's called Shark Island. Why? I don't know. We are sitting here in the middle of a forest on ground as solid as a rock. Actually, our initial assignment seems in a word "stupid." Our trainer asks us to sit down (on the ground?) and relax (with pine needles poking through my pants!). Next she says,

> Close your eyes and imagine that you are on a Caribbean cruise.

I fight my desire to peek. O.K., I say to myself, I can envision that. The air is cool, the wind is picking up, the boat is rocking gently.

> All of a sudden, wham! The boat hits a partially submerged island with the force of a torpedo, and you are taking in water fast! The captain says you have three minutes to get this entire team to the small speck of ground known as Shark Island.

I raise my hand and ask, "Why is it called Shark Island?"

> This is the breeding ground for the Great White Sharks. The dorsal fins have been spotted: the sharks are three minutes off and closing fast. They are definitely hungry.

19

I take some initiative, react quickly, jump to my feet, and say, "Where is the island?"

*The trainer points to a small, three-foot-square platform.*

Give me a break! We can't get twenty-four people on that island. Obviously, others have the same feelings. Fred, Larry, and Brenda all head for the middle of the island. I pull back and say, "Now just a minute. Can we talk about this arrangement?" I mean these folks are large enough to make "Hulk Hogan" look like one of the seven dwarfs. "This doesn't look fair and no one agreed to it." In the pit of my stomach, it feels like the survival of the fittest will be the law of the land for this team. Everyone else seems to draw the same conclusion.

We will have to coordinate if we are to survive. Now everyone starts talking, I mean everyone at the top of their voices. Mary finally screams, "Stop, stop, stop!! We have a minute and a half left. We have to get people on each other's shoulders." Two groups split off and come up with their own little plan while she is talking. A moment later we try for the island again, or I should say, some of us do. Mike must feel a compelling need to take a smoke break. I can't believe it; he just kicks back, gives up, with fifty-three seconds to go, but no one says anything to him.

Mary yells at me, "Lift someone up." Sure, if I can pick who it is. Why should I break my neck when Mike has checked out of this exercise? Now Mary yells, "Grab hands, everyone. Pull up on the count of three, at the same time." Now everyone is yelling. Our trainer says,

*Thirty seconds to go. The sharks are swarming.*

Sandy steps back and says, "It's impossible. There is no way this many people can fit on this island; some of us will have to be sacrificed." But no one volunteers except Sandy. Of course, Mike is enjoying his smoke break, but I guess he has sacrificed himself to the sharks. "Let's save all the people we can; everyone try to get one foot on, grab a hand, and pull hard." In one final attempt everyone gets set and...

*Time's up.*

What?

*Time is up.*

No way, we were all ready. I think we could do it; give us fifteen more seconds.

*No! Time is up.*

Shoot, right when we were ready, you robbed us of a victory. I think we could have done it (maybe). Everyone is ticked off–time, a pure technicality.

*Let's talk about this task. What happened here?*

Jerry speaks up first and says, "We tried our best, and we worked like a real team." "Yeah, given the size of the island, we did all right," Sandy chimes in. "Right on, we listened to everyone who had an idea." "Yeah, that was kind of fun." By now everyone is smiling and joking except our trainer, who looks at us with a steady poker face. Deep inside I sense she wants to push this discussion deeper, but first our trainer acknowledges our enthusiastic effort and gregarious group character.

*I think your energy was high; everyone had a lot of fun.*
*Did you achieve your objective on this task?*

For a moment, there is dead silence. Then, in a slightly defensive tone, someone says, "It all depends on how you define success."

*How do you define success?*

It is quiet again. "Well, if we were to experience the feeling of teamwork, then we did it here, but technically I guess you could say we didn't get everyone on the island, and the reason we didn't is because you called time's-up on us."

*So you are saying I'm the reason you didn't succeed?*

"Well, you called time's up and you gave us a scrawny little platform."

*Perhaps you're right. Maybe I did give you too big of a challenge.*

It is silent again. Bill responds, "No way, that's a poor excuse. I refuse to believe that the challenge was too big; nor was our trainer the reason for our failure."

*Talk more about that, Bill.*

"It didn't hit me at the time, but I don't think that we were a group. I saw the girls in one group and the men in two other separate groups. The only person we listened to was the person who yelled the loudest." Mary nods her head in agreement. Someone from our group then speaks up in a rather aggressive tone, "I think we were twenty-four teams here."

*What do you mean by that?*

Mike then comments, "Nobody was willing to listen to anybody else." Brenda then takes a turn, "Yeah, something has been bothering me, and it has been happening several times now. The men keep referring to the women as girls!" Linda supports her, "That's right. What's the deal, boys?"

Again, dead silence. Then Linda says, "We had to band together when we couldn't get you boys to listen to us." Bill barks back, "We tried to listen to your ideas." Brenda reacts quickly, "No way, it was a yelling contest." Someone else says, "You're full of baloney. Are you saying we are male chauvinists?"

*Time out, time out. It sounds like the women are not happy with their role. Has everyone heard that? Look, I think at this stage you need to just listen to each other, no attacking and no defending.*

"Just listen to each other. I don't think it was just the women who didn't get listened to. I know my ideas were not heard." Someone in the group responds sarcastically in the background, "Maybe you need to speak up a little louder."

*Time out. Remember what I said about the ground rules. Just listen to each other, no defending, no attacking.*

Fred takes the floor and says, "I have a question for Mike. Why did you stop participating halfway through this exercise?" Mike thinks a minute and then says, "I didn't stop." "Well it sure looked like you did when you sat down and lit up a cigarette." "Well, I just wasn't sure we had a good plan."

*Was Mike the only one who appeared to check out?*

"Well, at the very end, with only thirty seconds left, Sandy threw in the towel." Sandy responds, "That's when I knew it was impossible." "How in the hell did you know that! Woops...sorry, no attacking, I didn't mean it to sound that way." Fred looks at the trainer, "Why are you trying to turn our hard work and team effort into so much criticism? I mean this is a real downer."

*What I would like to do is focus on how you really worked together or didn't work together as a team. My job is to hold up the mirror and not to judge your work.*

"What do you think?"

> *I will be honest with you; it didn't seem like there was any serious participation. I don't know who really emerged as your leader. Few people were willing to defer to each other. I think the commitment was variable; some were heavily involved and some were passive. I'm not here to make you feel good or bad about this exercise, but rather to try to report accurately what seems to be happening and to get you to take a look at it, unless you don't want me to do that.*

"Look, I, for one, am here to learn all I can. I'm not getting my money's worth unless you are totally honest with me."

> *So, is everyone O.K. with that? I want to say a couple of things before we move on to another task. First, I believe that teamwork is a tricky topic to study and discuss. A lot of things go on and happen that are not really supportive of teamwork, and sometimes it's hard to put your finger on exactly what it is, but inside you know it doesn't feel right. Teamwork is something that has sort of a subliminal quality to it, so don't be afraid to speak up and act on your intuition or deep reactions and feelings if something about the team doesn't feel right or isn't working.*

> *Second, let's try not to confuse physical, athletic, or task success with the quality and success of the teamwork. You see, this team was very close to getting everyone on the island, and if you had all been pulling and working hard I think you would have succeeded, but succeeding in the physical sense was not the objective of this exercise or does anyone disagree?*

"I'm not sure exactly what you mean."

*If you had succeeded physically on this task, it would have been very difficult for you to examine teamwork carefully and clearly. I think everyone would have been caught up in the success of the moment. Sometimes in these activities, teams will succeed despite their best efforts to screw things up from a team or organizational perspective. Out here and in our own organizations back home, our raw energy and drive will carry us through some tasks. However, in other situations and when it is a close call, there is no question that teamwork will make all the difference in the world, in terms of achieving the final objective and personal job satisfaction. In my opinion, organizations are not just designed to achieve physical success. They are there to serve human needs, to be an outlet for self-expression, and to offer a sense of community and affiliation to members of the team. Oftentimes these individuals spend the best hours of their lives and dedicate their finest talents and efforts to the team's objectives. Teams are an important part of our lives, and it is rare that we are able to sit back and take a look at how we function and operate as a team. Does anyone have any questions or comments about this?*

Bill speaks up, "It sounds like you are saying we can be our own worst enemy and that we shot ourselves in the foot on this assignment."

*You know, Bill, one of your finest traits and the one that I admire most about you is your quick perceptiveness.*

Others respond and give Bill support for his willingness to make that observation.

# 3

# WHY NEW TEAMS STRUGGLE

We have observed countless groups struggle with activities such as Shark Island. The common denominator of these groups is that they are either all strangers or intact work teams and this is the first activity during which they are asked to work effectively together.

At least four issues inhibit these start-up groups from functioning as a team:

1. Task fixation, process blindness
2. Power struggles
3. Fight versus flight
4. Stereotyping

## TASK FIXATION, PROCESS BLINDNESS

Individual members justify any behavior as O.K. if it contributes to achieving the end product—successful completion of the task or the goal. Little to no concern is exhibited for how the group functioned during this journey toward their goal—the process. With this view, any means justify the end.

Shark Island magnifies task fixation by placing a three-minute time limit on the performance of the task. Thus, any means, like sacrificing team members, forming sub-groups to the exclusion of others, or not getting the commitment of all team members, are justified under the rubric of getting the task accomplished: "We had to do that to get the job done." Who can argue with success, even if there were casualties along the way? You can, if you were one of the casualties.

In a new group that is fixated totally on task success, individuals focus on their own needs to the exclusion of the needs of others. There is no support, recognition that individual differences are a potential benefit, deferring of egos, brainstorming, seeking commitment, or flexibility. However subtle or covert, a selfish competition is justified as necessary to expediently achieve the goal.

# POWER STRUGGLES

Internal conflicts make up part of the dynamics within a new group. Leadership: do we need a leader, who is going to lead, or will we follow the appointed leader? Teams asked to perform leaderless tasks such as Shark Island and volunteer groups struggle the most with issues of leadership. Groups relate to us that Shark Island would have been easier if we had appointed a leader. Having experimented with appointing a leader, we have observed that the group's behavior is the same. The only difference is that one person, the leader, is really frustrated by his/her inability to get the group's cooperation. The battle for influence and power continues.

Dominant individuals scramble to be recognized and influence others. Disagreements over ideas are positioned as win-lose alternatives. Accepting my ideas means rejecting yours. We have seen high-achieving executives' egos keep them from "dimming their headlights" and deferring to other team members.

Who's in and who's out is a conflict which often exists as a part of the dominant-individual struggle. Cliques, groups within groups, and "we" versus "them" are terms used to describe this situation. In new groups this struggle is fostered by the need to find someone who will support your ideas. Once found, the divisiveness of positioning or lobbying for a majority vote starts. The "outs" resent the "ins" and will resist their ideas, sabotage their plans, or simply refuse to be fully functioning members of the team.

## FIGHT OR FLIGHT

During Shark Island, the following fight or flight behaviors have been observed:

- Unwillingness to listen to others
- Fear of speaking up or fighting for a position
- Low trust in other members, causing withdrawal
- Taking the task too lightly
- Little group planning
- Non-involvement
- Silence as preferable to vulnerability

Regardless of the behavior, the result is the same: the team loses resources, energy, and creativity. Decisions are made and plans are implemented with less than total group input and support. It is frustrating to be a team member when fight or flight behavior is exhibited. Unless the team is organizationally mandated to remain in existence, this dissatisfaction and frustration among the members will cause it to perish.

## STEREOTYPING

New groups are particularly susceptible to this struggle–are individual differences recognized and taken into consideration, or are generalizations about motives and behaviors made about the members of a group?

During Shark Island, stereotypes about male/female roles often emerge. More often than not, females are given a secondary role, not allowed to perform physical tasks like lifting others, and listened to only as a last resort. A more subtle stereotyping occurs when physical size is equated with strength, balance, and athletic agility. The largest male is often forced into the position of lifting, carrying, or pulling others when activities later in the program prove this stereotype that equates size with strength to be false.

We are constantly amazed, after only a brief introduction, how quickly generalizations are made about individuals. These stereotypes serve as blinders and keep the group from using all the resources available to the team.

## ACTION ITEMS FOR START-UP TEAMS

**1.     Jointly define how the group will function.**

The challenge for a new group is to establish a way of operating that will allow process issues to be noticed, discussed, and taken into account as the group works on the tasks to be accomplished. New groups could profitably invest time in talking about some key issues:

- How should we function as a group
- How should we make decisions
- What do we expect from one another
- How will we monitor our process so that it doesn't become a problem

Groups that become cohesive and maintain effective teamwork balance their attention to task and process issues. Effective team members do not fixate on either; they monitor both and openly discuss needed improvements.

## 2. Create a win-win atmosphere.

When teams are functioning effectively, disagreements or differing views are explored not to declare one view the winner, but to seek the best decision. Every reader has been on a team where the free flow of information has created not a win-lose environment but an environment encouraging discussion that leads to a decision which is better than any of the original positions presented.

The group will go through a phase when power struggles predominate unless the leader or a team member establishes the mode of operation and has the courage to point out when power struggles are occurring within the team.

Functioning teams realize that leadership can shift from one to another member of the team depending on the task at hand. The designated leader knows that leadership can be shared or transferred without a loss of power.

## 3. Manage fight or flight behavior.

Teamwork means managing fight or flight behaviors so they do not become counterproductive. All members take the responsibility for monitoring these behaviors and focusing the group's attention on resolving them when they occur.

## 4. Test out your assumptions about team members.

Teamwork demands clarity with regard to what each member wants, needs, and is willing to do. No assumptions are made or left unchecked. Profitable time can be spent discussing each team member's answers to these three questions:

> A. What should other team members do more of because it helps me be a more productive team member?

B. What should other team members stop doing
because it hinders my productivity and
contribution as a team member?

C. What should other team members start doing
because this will help me be a more active and
contributing member of this team?

This process will clarify the various roles of team members and
prevent stereotypes and assumptions from determining the group's
behavior.

# 4
# BEWARE OF ACID RIVER

What a crummy day-cold, overcast with the threat of precipitation, and windy. I wish someone would tell me when I'm having fun. Our twelve-person group has been walking from base camp now for about five minutes. Great, we seem to be slowing down. What's that? The facilitator is telling the group to gather around for our instructions.

The facilitator is standing on the bank of a muddy pond. Here she goes with another one of those corny stories:

> *Your group is being doggedly followed by a group of escaped death-row convicts. Your only chance of alluding this group is for all twelve of you to get across to the shore behind me. There you will find all terrain vehicles to transport you quickly and safely out of reach of your followers. The only catch is that the pond is really acid and if any part of you or your supplies touch this acid, severe penalties will result. The only safe places are the posts sticking out of the water and the island. You cannot use the pond bank. Your supplies are the three boards and 15 feet of rope over there. You have 45 minutes to get your entire group safely to the island before the convicts arrive. Be advised that you do not want to meet, let alone be held hostage by, the convicts. Any questions?*

The group looks out over the pond and sees the following situation:

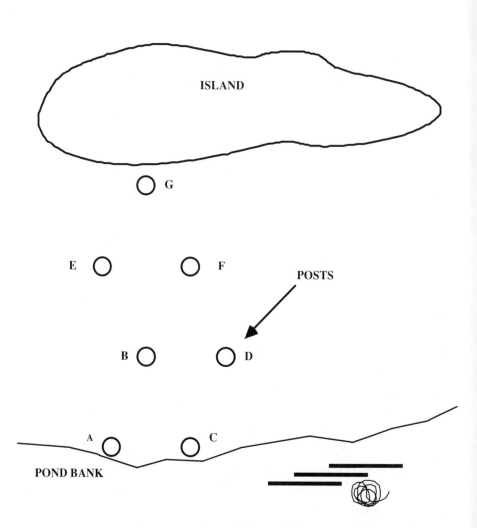

There are no questions, so the facilitator starts the 45-minute clock. My first reaction is that the water looks awfully cold, and the smell of decomposing leaves makes me feel that the bottom should be real gooey.

Tuning back to the conversation around me, at least three small groups of people seem to be doing different things. Three of the guys are looking at the boards and getting ready to try and place one from Post A to B. Another small group is looking out over the water, seemingly studying the way the posts are set up. The third group, including myself, is just kind of milling around, not knowing what to do or where to start. George, mister macho, picks up a board and heads for Post A.

Sheila yells, "Where in the H_ _ _ do you think you're going with that board?" George returns the compliment by saying, "I'm going to get something done so we can get out of this cold and back to base camp." I can't help thinking I've seen this movie before. George is out for himself, and if you want to join him, fine. If not, fine also, but just stay out of his way. Sheila steps in front of George saying, "Hold it! We need to figure out how to go about this project and develop a plan of action. I suggest we appoint a leader to coordinate our efforts."

George sidesteps her saying, "You've got the action part right. I, for one, am going to get to the island. If anyone wants to help, let's get going." Three other guys step forward, and they place one end of the board on Post A. George ties the rope to the other end, and they are in the process of lowering it to Post B when Mary states, "It's too short; you're not going to make it. The board will go into the acid." George looks at her in disbelief and asks Bill to hold the rope so he can step aside and see if she's right. Looking at the board and judging the distance, George concedes that she may be right, that it won't reach. "Haul it back in," he commands, "I'll have to think of something else."

Sheila and five other group members have stepped back from the bank and are using the ground and small pieces of sticks to try out different plans. Sheila suggests that this group take about 15 minutes brainstorming various alternatives. Bill is standing next to me and says, "I think the board will reach from post A to post C; then we can T another board to Point B." I look at him as if to say "T a board-just like an engineer," but instead mumble, "That could be an alternative." Rather than try and understand what Bill is suggesting, I ask, "Does anyone know how much time we have left?" The total silence is answer enough. The facilitator just says,

*I think I hear some loud yelling in the distance. Voices sure do travel a long way in the mountains.*

Sheila asks me to keep time from this point forward and let them know when fifteen minutes have passed. All of the group except George and three other guys seems to be interested in Sheila's approach. George just states, "That's just like you staff people–study the project to death. We need to tie two boards together and get going." Setting my watch, I notice that Bill has just sat down under a tree and looks like he could go to sleep. I'm kind of torn as to whether to stay with Sheila, go help George, or ask Bill what's the matter. In my moment of indecision, I get the impression that I'm in the middle of a three-ring circus. Little do I know that things will get worse before they get better.

George has just connected Post A with Post B via a shaky-looking bridge of the two tied boards. He starts to walk out onto the boards when Sheila asks, "George, what if you lose those two boards in the acid? Where will the rest of us be?"

George just smiles and says, "Probably still sitting there talking about things. At least I will have tried something." He then asks one of his other guys to bring the third board to him once he gets to Post B. When George and Hank arrive at Point B they try to wrestle the third board out to Post F. Both of them lose their balance and go into the acid. I think the two feet of mud below the acid is worse than having fallen in the water. The facilitator asks George and Hank to return to the bank, with all the supplies, and from this point forward they are required to be mute.

Sheila asks Mary to get the third board from George and place it on the ground so we can all see the exact length. George begrudgingly gives her the board and starts, in silence, to get the three guys he has been working with to connect Post A and B using the two boards that are still tied together.

I am amazed how determined George is, even though he can't talk. Or is it pig-headed? He is gently shoving and pointing to the other three, who also are not talking, even though they can. From the look on his face, I would bet nothing could change or influence his thinking–his mind is set. In fact I would be afraid to try. No wonder so few people are excited when they have to work with George on a project: he treats everyone as a pair of hands with no important ideas or thoughts to contribute.

I tell Sheila that fifteen minutes has passed, and she says, "Then we agree that the best way is to put a board from Post A to Post C." Bill, still sitting under a tree, just smiles and shakes his head. George and Hank are again at Point B, struggling to lift up the two boards and lower them to post F.

Sheila asks George if he would be willing to try another way. George, soaking wet and covered with mud, just looks at her in disbelief; and even without being able to talk, the message is clear. As he turns toward Hank, he again loses his balance and both he and Hank take another dip into the acid. The facilitator says,

> *George, you and Hank take all the supplies back to the bank, and for your penalty you both can talk and Sheila is muted.*

As I look at Sheila, I am struck by how puzzled and beaten she looks. She just gives a shrug and withdraws to the outside of the group. George yells, "Great, now let's get these two boards tied together and put them from Post A to B." I ask, "How are we all going to get across on two boards?" George says, "Simple; we will go across in two's. Two people can stand on a post and lower the two boards from Post B to F. Then, they can take the third board and slide it out on the two boards just far enough so it reaches Post G, where one person can jump to the bank."

All at once a number of complaints and statements of disbelief are expressed. Mary asks, "What about the other plan?" George just says, "Since I am the strongest, I suggest that Hank and I go out first. I will stay at Point F and move the two boards back to Post B, then A, where I will pick up another member of the group and take him/her across. Bill says, in a very loud voice, "That is the worst approach I can think of. Why not try the approach suggested by the people working with Sheila?" Sheila starts to come forward but is stopped when George says, "That's a good fall-back plan," while he and Hank shoulder the two tied boards and head for Post A.

The group looks on in disgust and disbelief as George and Hank try to make their idea work. After falling off of Post B for the third time, the facilitator just asks them to take the supplies back to the bank and start again. I am amazed that when they fall in, the rest of the group applauds. George stands on the bank and says, "O.K., Hank, let's try it again. We'll show them."

Bill grabs George's shoulders and not so gently spins him around, saying, "I'm taking over; you go sit down." I don't think I've ever seen Bill so mad. The group just stares at Bill in quiet disbelief. As he's sitting down, George says, "That's what I thought–not a better idea in the group, or are you all mute? Bill starts to say something that I know he will regret when the facilitator says,

> *Time's up. The convicts now have you as hostages and will show you the type of games they like to play.*

# 5
# WHY WE FAILED AT ACID RIVER

Sitting by this pond with our facilitator discussing why a group of twelve adults couldn't accomplish a simple task is embarrassing. We have looked at the model we developed for how effective teams function and found ourselves wanting in every area. It sounded so simple when we were talking about it this morning, but we sure couldn't do it this afternoon.

About the only saving note is that our managers didn't see this exhibition. This will not happen again, or at least I won't be a part of it. Everyone is just looking at the ground. What a humbling experience.

The facilitator concludes,

> O.K. I think we have beaten this one enough. I want you to spend time recording your thoughts and the actions you will take in your journals. I am going back to the administrative building. Dinner will be served in one hour.

As the facilitator walks off, I am struck with the fact that no one is moving or talking–just staring at the ground or out over the pond. We have been defeated, and my guess is that no one feels good or proud of his/her behavior.

I can't stand it any longer, so I ask, "Is anybody else as ticked and embarrassed as I am? I think we need to talk and get our stuff together—we have two more days of this, and right now I can't say I'm looking forward to working with this group. As a start, I thought our team stunk, and I'm frustrated and mad!"

Silence! Sheila is the first to talk. "If any of our teams back at work did what we just did, we would fire them. And if I were my manager, I would seriously question my leadership ability. George, I am infuriated with you."

George, in a condescending tone, responds, "Hey, Sheila, chill out. This is just a game. No big deal."

Bill jumps to his feet and says, "George, you're lying! If this was not important to you, why were you such a bull-headed jerk about your ideas—no one else fell in the water as many times as you did."

"Hey, Bill, sit on it! You're the one who checked out; at least I hung in there until the end. Next time, why don't you lead?"

Before Bill can respond, I put my hands together forming a time-out signal and say, "Here we go again, just like our facilitator pointed out—we're real good at defending our position and attacking others and poor in our problem-solving efforts. Let's act like the successful managers we are and talk about what we need to do to get better. I don't have the time to sit and listen to George argue with everyone. What do you think, Bill?"

Bill rolls his eyes toward the top of his head and laughs, "We talked about this with the facilitator. Want me to rattle off all the things we didn't do?"

Sheila says, "That might be a start, to see if we all agree or whether we were just being nice when the facilitator was here. I don't think

George agreed with what was being said during our debrief of the exercise."

"I'm willing to listen to Bill's list," responds George.

"Listen? That will be a first for you, George," snaps Bill. "O.K., here is what I wrote down as we were talking about our approach to this event:

>    We didn't do any planning–our facilitator called us the Ready, Fire, Aim gang.

>    We weren't in agreement on what our goal or objective was."

Mary asks, "Who thinks we weren't trying to get the entire team across the pond as safely as possible?"

Sheila responds, "I think the majority would agree we were trying, but I believe George and his followers were in it for themselves and were trying to show the rest of us or the facilitator that they could succeed without our help."

All eyes turn to George, who says, "So what's the matter with winning? I like to win and know that I can do whatever I set my mind to."

Shaking my head I counter, "George, no one won here. Even if you and your followers had made it across the pond, the entire team would have lost. Can't you see that? Why do you think we applauded when you fell in the pond?"

George just sits there and shrugs his shoulders. Finally he interjects, "My followers? What about Sheila's followers? What about the rest who didn't follow at all? In my opinion, we were at least three groups, not just one."

Bill nods, "That fits with the next two points I wrote down. Let me read the rest of the things we didn't do.

> We didn't have a clear leader whom everyone would follow. Sheila and George were competing for this honor.

> We didn't listen to each other. Some good ideas were never given serious consideration. Our problem-solving sucks."

George nods, "Like I said, groups within a group–us versus us."

Bill adds, "Don't lose sight of our poor listening and problem-solving. I, for one, know my idea of the T was passed over. That's O.K., the group didn't have to buy it, but at least you could have heard me out. I design and build things for a living. This challenge is no different from similar construction projects I have been involved with."

"Why didn't you tell us that?" I ask.

"No one asked. Besides, that is just my own example. There were others whose ideas and suggestions never got a fair trial. For me, the issue is not that my idea didn't get used; the frustration is that we didn't get all the ideas out on the table. The loudest or most aggressive person's ideas were used. I don't call that real creative," responds Bill. "That ties in with the next item I wrote down.

> We didn't openly express both our ideas and feelings.

I couldn't have been the only person who was angry with George–but I didn't say anything."

Another team member agrees. "You're right. I held my thoughts and feelings inside–figured, what good would it do anyway. But, that's my problem; I have to take more responsibility for fairly representing myself in this group. What else have you got on your list, Bill?"

"A couple of other points,

> Not everyone was committed to the approach—some people checked out. And finally,"

"Hold it!" I say. "Why did you check out, Bill?"

Tentatively Bill responds, "I was mad. You didn't want to listen to my ideas so I concluded, 'To hell with you—go ahead and fail.' Not a very mature reaction, but there it is. If you want me to be involved, give me the courtesy of listening to me."

Conrad adds, "I checked out because I didn't want to have to fight to be recognized. George and Sheila were in control, and the rest of us were either in one camp or the other. I was on the fence, not committed to either, and no efforts were made to ask my opinion. I zoned out–didn't care what happened."

Laughingly, Bill blurts out, "That is close to my last point; the rest of you are going to think Conrad is my straight man. Here is how I put it:

> We weren't very good followers. More than one person wasn't willing to dim their headlights and follow. Others weren't given the opportunity to lead.

That about does it. Not a pretty picture."

George says, "All right. So now that we know what we didn't do— so what?"

Sheila addresses the group, "Any disagreements with what Bill has said? George?"

George just looks around the group, then slowly shakes his head from side to side saying, "No, but I don't know if I wouldn't do the same thing again. Still, if you all think there is a better way, I'm willing to try."

Sheila looks at George and then cautiously says, "If we don't figure out a better way, we'll never be a team. The challenges they throw at us over the next two days will be a continuation of what we just went through. How many want two more days of this?"

No one raises a hand.

"I started this discussion, and I don't! How many think we can agree on what to do differently next time?"

Hands shoot up, and the vote is unanimous.

Mary has been sitting quietly. "I have been listening and taking my own notes. Here's what I think we need to commit to doing if we have another group task to accomplish:

> Find out if anyone has had a similar experience and, if so, appoint that person the leader. If not, the team needs to agree on who will be the leader.
>
> The leader needs to figure out how to involve all of us in brainstorming ideas and working through our plan of action.
>
> Everyone needs to take responsibility to participate, to communicate suggestions, reservations, and true feelings.
>
> Once we agree on what we are going to do, everyone, and I mean everyone, gets 100% involved in implementing our plan."

Members of the team start talking, "Yeah." "Right on." "Let's do it." "We'll show our facilitator how it's done." "We can do it."

I can feel the energy level and excitement in the group increasing. Even George seems to be excited. Sheila moves to the center of the group, puts her hand out, and says, "What do you say, team, can we do it?"

Other team members place their hands on hers and a loud, collective **"YES!"** echoes through the valley.

# 6

# TWO TEAMS PASSING IN THE DARK

What a lousy day, rainy and overcast. In a van are six people, joking and having a good time as they wind their way down the canyon. About 2 miles away from base camp, each member of the team receives the following written instructions:

## CAVE SCENARIO

Members of your organization have agreed to participate in a planning and goal setting meeting. A proposal was made and accepted to meet at an off-site, remote location that will enable your group to achieve maximum creativity and communication. Your journey begins as a rather uneventful event. The motion of the van as it winds its way through the mountains combined with the warm sun, causes you to drift off for a pleasant nap.

The next thing you remember hearing is the screeching brakes of the van. As you struggle to open your eyes, the silence in the van is broken by the chatter of questions: What is it? Why are we stopping? What is the problem?

Much to your amazement, you see a school teacher and a group of students standing on the highway, forcing your van to stop. There is no question that some emergency or crisis has occurred. The

47

tingling up and down your spine confirms your fears. The information that you gather from the panic-stricken teacher is skimpy at best but consists of the following facts:

1.  The teacher was conducting a science field trip with twelve children. They were exploring a cave just yards from where you are now.

2.  For some unknown reason, one of the twelve children has become lost in the cave and may possibly be injured.

3.  The teacher and remaining children fled from the cave to obtain emergency assistance to rescue the child.

4.  The teacher can provide only an approximate description of the cave and a general location of the child (a crude map is available).

5.  Unfortunately, the teacher is much too nervous to actually assist in a possible rescue attempt. Information from the children is confusing and unreliable.

6.  The teacher and children have been in the cave all morning.

Your conclusion is that your team is the only group available to help, and you are on your own to develop a plan for the rescue effort.

# YOUR TASK

Your team has volunteered to attempt a rescue of the lost and possibly injured child. You have been able to assemble a limited amount of equipment and resources to assist in accomplishing the task. Your task, is first, to individually rank order the twenty resources listed on the attached sheet according to their importance in facilitating a safe and successful rescue. The most important item should receive a rank of 1, the least important a rank of 20. Once you have completed your individual rankings, the team must come up with a group ranking of the resources.

# RESOURCE LIST

Crude map

Jackknife

Plastic liners to protect feet from moisture

Drinking water

Protective head gear

Bat fumigant

Compass

Small "army" shovel

First aid kit

Pitons (anchors for climbing)

Roll of string

Two candles

Five matches

Chalk

Small quantity of high-energy food/snacks

Rock hammer

Blanket

Climbing rope with figure-8 break device

Rescue litter

# OPERATING ASSUMPTIONS

1. The people on your team are the people who will actually attempt the rescue mission.

2. The team you are on has agreed to stick together.

3. One usable flashlight was dropped in the cave by a child, and the only other flashlight contains batteries that are too weak to be used.

4. All items on your resource list are in good condition.

5. It is possible, but unlikely that other parties are exploring the cave at the present time.

6. Additional rescue help is miles away, and you will have to rely on the skills and abilities within your own team to execute the rescue.

A healthy debate ensues as team members argue that certain items on the resource list should receive a higher ranking than others. The final decision is made, and the trainer then informs the group that they will be able to take only the top six items from their list on the rescue mission.

"You mean we are actually going into the cave?"

The van pulls over and members slowly get out, putting on their safety helmets while glancing at the water cascading down a fifty-yard embankment from the mouth of a cave. They are issued the chosen resources: two candles, five matches, a crude map of the cave, chalk, a compass, and a ball of string. As they climb the embankment, a few members start to shiver and rub their arms together, to compensate for the too-few clothes they have for this damp and cold day.

Once at the mouth of the cave, the group divides the tasks to be performed during the journey: map reader, candle holder, navigator and course marker, leader, and supporters. Because of David's military background, his ability to dominate the discussions, and the fact that no one on the team has ever been in a cave before, he is halfheartedly asked to lead.

After a brief discussion, the team, along with their trainer, marches single file into the darkness of the cave. Even the casual observer can see a great deal of reservation and trepidation within the team. They have decided to go as far as the ball of string will permit and then make a decision.

Sixty yards later they are at the end of their string, and from the single candle at the front, the shadowy outline of a large rock fall looms like a watchdog meant to keep travelers from going beyond this point. The chirping of bats can be heard as they wing their way through the dark to some unknown destiny. In the distance the sound of running water encroaches on the absolute silence, broken only by the moans from hitting an elbow or knee on a protruding rock ledge.

The journey has been awkward and slow. Those at the front have limited sight, while the rear of the line is completely in the dark. A few members have sped forward only to be yelled back by the main group. David has tried to speed up the pace to no avail. In disgust, he suggests that some of the faster members of the team take the supplies and move ahead while the others rest and set up an intermediate camp here at the base of the rock fall.

The group circles around the candle for the shortest team meeting on record. Over protests from the speed burners, they agree to

drop the string and complete the rescue as a total group. David moves out of the lead position to the middle of the line.
**Score: Team = 1, Individuals = 0.**

The next forty-five minutes are spent climbing up and over two more rock slides, duck walking for twenty yards along a narrow passage, and wading through a narrow channel on slippery rocks in thigh-deep, thirty-five-degree mountain water. As they stand in the water, exhaustion, frustration, and darkness seems to be winning. They huddle around one another and vote to continue until the candle gives out. The hesitation and trepidation have been replaced by a unified resolve and commitment–to find the child.
**Score: Team = 2, Individuals = 0.**

Doggedly they trudge forward, approaching an island. Scrambling, pulling each other out of the water, they discover a doll lying next to a new flashlight hidden in the cracks. "The kid, I can't believe we found the kid." "We did it." Passing the doll from member to member, the congratulations and cheers fill the silence one-half mile into the cave.

"Let's get the hell out of here" seems to jump from more than one throat. Suddenly, a dull reflection from a foreign light source bounces off the surface of the water. Someone or something is coming toward the island, mysteriously following the same path the team has just traversed. Necks and eyes strain to cut through the darkness.

"Who goes there? . . . I said, who are you?"

"We are a team trying to find and rescue a lost child."

From the island is blurted, "We have found the child. Turn back."

But the light keeps coming, dancing off the water and sides of the cave. Slosh, slosh, slosh, ever moving forward. Faces can now be seen as the group approaches the island. Standing in the water, the leader asks, "How many kids did you find?"

"One!"

"One?" There is another lost kid in the cave, and we need to rescue both kids."

"The teacher said one child, and we have found her. Too bad, you're late."

"But I tell you, there is another child lost in here."

The team on the island caucuses and issues their decision: "We have found our kid and are going out: find your own kid." The team on the island watches, not yielding any of their hard-won dry land. The message is clear: Don't challenge us.
**Score: My Team = 1, Total Team = 0.**

Shivering from standing in the cold water is replaced by a rise in body temperature and tempers. "At least give us your flashlight since we have used up one of our candles." This request is met with silent stares. "How about letting the more athletic people from each team go forward and find the second child while the rest of us get out of here? If we pool our resources, both teams can get out of here faster and accomplish a total rescue."

"We don't have to negotiate. We're going out," yells David.

"Look, some members of our team are scared, tired, and cold–they need to go out."

From the back of the island comes, "Does it look like we're sweating? We'll take care of ourselves; you guys should do the same. You're just trying to trick us."

"Come on. It's cold in this water; someone make a decision."

"We have," snaps David as he jumps off the island. "We're heading out." In unison, the other team members follow with lighted candle, flashlight, and doll. David's parting shot cuts through the dark right to the heart of the other team, "We all know the rules; we did our job." Their lights grow dimmer and dimmer until the second team is left standing in the shadows of their one remaining candle.
**Score: My Team = 2, Total Team = 0.**

"To hell with them. I guess it's every team for themselves."

"You bet, I can't believe they were so pigheaded."

With new resolve, the second team and it's trainer move forward into the darkness in search of the second child. Only the trainer knows the risks they have assumed. The comments within the team indicate that finding the child is secondary to showing the other team that they don't need their help. A consensus starts to form that the winner will be the team that finds the second child and that the first team out will have failed. "What a bunch of losers the first team is. Serves them right!"

With bitter determination they traverse over another rock slide, climb through a waterfall, and find the second child 300 yards from the island. Guarding the remaining one-half candle, they take their short-lived victory and race toward the safety of the mouth of the cave.

"Wait until I get a hold of David . . . what a scumbag."

"I'd have thought the personnel guy would have been more understanding."

"Birds of a feather . . . . I don't even want to talk to them. We're number one."

"We're number one.  We're number one."

"Ouch, d_ _n rocks.  Thanks!  I'm O.K., let's keep moving."

**Score:  My Team = 3, Total Team = 0.**

At first it is just a faint change; then the team starts to recognize that more light is coming in.  Then, it's definite: they have made it.  The light from the outside bathes the rocks, and the team bursts out on a grey overcast sky.  To them, the sky looks as inviting and welcome as an evening sunset.

No celebration, no congratulations.  The first team is waiting as the second team emerges from the cave, first with grins, then with sneers as they see their welcoming party.

"We won."

"The hell you did!" snaps David.

**Final Score:  My Team = 4, Total Team = 0.**

The teams are at odds and have only one thing in common:  they both have rescued a child and the symbolic doll has become the center of their attention.

The two trainers and safety technicians take off their helmets.

*Everyone be seated.  I think both two teams have a lot to talk about.*

# 7

# EXPERTS DISCUSS THE CAVE

Having just gone through the rescue mission with the two teams a panel of "experts" discusses their observations. The panel represents three unique perspectives:

- Penelope Harriet-Daniels **(PHD)**, Professor of Organization Behavior, Center For Group Development
- Clarence Eugene Olifant **(CEO)**, Retired Chief Executive Officer
- Harold Reginald Crandall **(HRC),** Human Resource Consultant

HRC:   What we have just observed in the cave is typical behavior when two teams are given the opportunity to act as one. Why do you think these two teams competed with one another instead of cooperating?

PHD:   That is rather obvious. Each team defined its mission in terms beating the other team, even though they were trying to accomplish the same goal. Cohesion within the team built as the team members overcame adversity. They closed ranks and didn't allow the other team in. My team became "good"; your team was "bad."

CEO:   I have seen the same phenomenon when it comes to departments within a company: Sales vs. Production, Maintenance vs. Production, Personnel vs. Finance, Finance vs. Everyone. I have been constantly amazed at how this "we versus them" attitude develops so fast.

PHD:   Come now, it is natural for each team to believe that it's solution/approach is "best" and to downgrade or reject the other team's solution.

CEO:   Competition is what made America great. I surely wouldn't want a department head to think her unit is second best. Winning and striving to win keeps everybody on their toes. But these teams outwardly attacked and treated the other team as adversaries–that's going a bit too far.

HRC:   Who won in this event?

PHD:   In my opinion, both teams think they did. Each accomplished it's goal; each rescued a child. I also see them treating members of the other team as losers. The whole atmosphere at the end of the event was distorted–no cheering because both teams won. Self-congratulation prevailed.

CEO:   You're making too much out of this. Healthy competition produces results. Both teams were driven to accomplish their mission. Both are winners.

HRC:   How come they don't act like winners, then?

PHD:   This is classical behavior. Each team made unfounded assumptions about the other team's position. Individuals on the first team thought members of the second team were lying about the second child to gain an advantage over them. The second team assumed the first team's motives were to win, to be first out of the cave at the expense of the second team. Based on these assumptions, individual team members chose not to share information and resources. The other team became the enemy.

CEO:     I did hear a lot of caustic remarks about the other team and team members. What-ever was gained by them competing could prove to be costly if these two teams had to cooperate in the future. They would fight it out like cats and dogs. I don't think it's an overstatement that outright dislike exists between members of the two teams.

HRC:     O.K., so we all have seen the end result of these two teams competing with one another. What I'd like to hear is your views on why the situation degenerated to its present state. Is it just human nature?

CEO:     People cooperate with each other all the time. We couldn't have organizations or get complex jobs done if they didn't. No, I have a much brighter view of human nature.

PHD:     Let me see if I can simplify this. First, our studies show that uncooperativeness is not a condition of the human animal. What we have to look at is what each team perceived to be the conditions under which it was working.

CEO:     You mean in a cave?

PHD:     No, the cave just served to magnify certain conditions. Our university has sponsored a very sophisticated and in-depth study of groups under conditions where competition and cooperation are possibilities. I can send each of you a copy of the report, if you would like.

HRC: I would rather hear a concise description, if you don't mind.

PHD: I'll try not to get too technical. What we have found that the things that foster competition and destroy cooperation are:

- No pressure or opportunities for the groups to cooperate
- Low trust between the groups
- Lack of a superordinate goal

CEO: What do you mean by that?

HRC: To me, it means the two teams did not have a common goal; each had its own goal, and this is all the team members concentrated on achieving.

PHD: You must be more precise. A superordinate goal is one for which attainment goes beyond the resources and efforts of the separate groups alone–they must cooperate.

CEO: In the cave there was no need to cooperate. Each group had the resources to achieve its individual goals, just like some departments I know.

PHD: If I may continue, additional factors also contributed to the groups competing with one another:

- An unwillingness or inability to have open communications
- High cohesion within each team

- A belief in the basic goodness or
  righteousness of the group
- A scarcity of rewards
- A sense of urgency

HRC: The team members sure were anxious to get out of the cave. So by keeping them apart, yet letting them feel a sense of achievement as they faced the adversity of surviving in the cave and enabling one group to get the reward (doll) first, you're saying the outcome was inevitable?

PHD: To be scientifically correct, under these conditions, a significantly higher probability exists that competition between the groups will occur.

CEO: Don't give me that probability mumbo jumbo. That's like saying you're a little bit pregnant. The bottom line is they didn't work together. Let me put it in practical terms, Professor. If I want two or more departments to work together as one unit, they need to:

- Have a goal which will require their
  cooperation
- Talk openly to each other
- Mix up the work so that different
  departments confront tasks together
- Spread the pay and praise out to the
  entire unit, not the individual
  departments

PHD: I haven't finished reporting our findings. The last thing we found that contributed to competition was when the individual team leader saw his/her role as protecting the team and making sure his/her team got the best deal. I call it the **The Guardian Syndrome**.

HRC:    So to CEO's list, we should add that the team leaders must be held accountable for the amount of cooperation between their teams.

CEO:    I can understand that, but it sure is a different way of operating. Under the Management By Objective system we used in our firm, objectives were, for the most part individual, with a few department-wide objectives. I cannot recall asking individuals to base their performance objectives on the level of cooperation that existed between their department and those they had to work with.

PHD:    It is little wonder, then, that you probably had very strong departments competing with one another for the corporate limelight, but little cross-department cooperation and collaboration.

CEO:    I'll be the judge of that!

HRC:    PHD, let's restrict our comments to the two teams in the cave, O.K.?

PHD:    Just trying to shed a little light on things, old boy. I can live with that restriction, besides, that concludes the non-methodological findings of our studies. Can I answer any additional questions?

CEO:    Just one. If you were in charge of these two teams, what would you do now?

PHD:    In charge, uh, well, uh . . .

HRC:    Let me take a stab at it. I would ask them to meet as one team and openly discuss what each team sees the other doing, to both foster the competition and keep the teams from cooperating. Then, I would help them establish specific actions that they could buy into as steps for becoming more cooperative. Lastly, I would make sure that a process was in place to help the entire group monitor how well it is doing and where changes need to be made to become more cooperative.

**CEO:** Maybe I don't understand, but in plain English I would tell them that I expect them to cooperate, and if they can't I will find some people who can.

**PHD:** I think both approaches have merit. It would be interesting to study which is more effective. Both of you have forgotten the most important motivating factor in the area of cooperation—**superordinate goals.** That's one thing I make sure my freshman students remember.

"Well, if that is all, gentlemen, I have to get back to campus for my graduate seminar on Research Methodology."

Stuffing her notes into her backpack, PHD bicycled off, leaving CEO and HRC to ponder the lessons learned from the cave event.

# 8

# IF YOU COULD TALK TOTHE ANIMALS—BOAT BUILDING

During a team activity horses, deer, cattle, moose, or squirrels often stand at a distance contentedly observing. We have often wondered, if they could talk, what they would say. Perhaps it would be a scene something like this ...

Today was the day that Cleo and Napoleon had been anticipating for many weeks, the word had spread throughout the ranch that **humans** were coming. Cleo and Napoleon had been designated to proceed to the large pond, observe the extraordinary events and report to the rest of the animals. Rumors were rampant regarding what these humans might be up to: buy the ranch, a fishing trip, just a picnic, or a training activity. The whole thing seemed mysterious, and Cleo and Napoleon walked to the pond together, cautious and untrusting of the humans.

Cleo and Napoleon were an odd sight. Cleo was a huge beast–a hard working horse, stout and reliable. She's been bred to handle the toughest manual labor that Harry Mossback had on the ranch, and she rarely complained. Cleo's features were rough, huge feet and broad shoulders, Napoleon, on the other hand, was slick, with fine lines and the grooming customary for show horses of Napoleon's caliber. Napoleon was rather annoyed when he found out that the big event would start at 8:00 a.m. as he was normally just  getting up at this time of day.  Cleo, on the other hand, had already put in two hours of work and relished the day off as a rare treat in light of her usual six-day work weeks.

Arriving at the pond about the same time as the humans, Cleo and Napoleon both looked inconspicuous enough as they inched their way closer to the action.  Both sensed the impending excitement and electricity in the air, and they didn't want to miss the action. The humans, for the most part, seemed curious but initially confused by their assigned task.  For some reason, many people were lamenting the necessity of coming out to the large pond in the first place.  One human was overheard to say, "Now what are these instructors up to?  With no explanation they tell us to report to the edge of the big pond near the maple tree, and that's it.  No more communication.  They didn't ever tell us what our job would be once we got here."

Cleo smiled to herself as Napoleon munched on some tender grass shoots that grew near the pond. She then spoke softly, "You know, Napoleon, I hear the animals all over the ranch say the same thing about Mr. Mossback.  It seems like we never know what he wants from day to day or what our real goal is here on the farm. One day I am plowing a field, and then before you know it we are off pulling up old tree stumps or something else before the fields are done. Sometimes it feels like a big activity trap."

Surprised at Cleo's boldness, Napoleon responded,  "Cleo, Mr. Mossback is a very busy person.  He doesn't always have the time to keep everyone informed and feeling good about where we are going with the ranch. The ranch mortgage payment has to be made every quarter.  That is a heavy responsibility and has to come before he takes time with us. The leaders want quick results now. In other words, no one really cares about or appreciates the working animal!"

Cleo knows it's no use arguing with Napoleon on this point because he always defends Mossback. Admittedly the responsibility of running a big ranch is enormous and creates a lot of pressure. However, Cleo and most of the other animals had felt for years that if the priorities, goals, and future direction for the ranch were explained, everyone could work more effectively towards those goals.

At last , someone who seemed to be in charge stepped forward with a piece of paper in hand and said to the group,

> *"Here is your mission. You will be divided into two teams: Green and Red. Each team will **DESIGN, CONSTRUCT, AND SAFELY FLOAT** a raft that will hold all of the team members from here to a point directly opposite on the other shore. All team members will be required to ride on the raft. Your goal is to keep everyone safe and as dry as possible. Everyone must wear a life jacket. The only construction materials you have to construct the boat are as follows:*
>
> > 2  *large drums*
> > 5  *sections of styrofoam*
> > 1  *inner tube*
> > 3  *pieces of lumber*
> > 25 *feet of rope*
> > 1  *plastic tarp/canvas*
>
> *A working drawing must be submitted in 30 minutes. You may now begin the designing process."*

Napoleon was especially doubtful that a raft could be built which would hold an entire team of humans without sinking. This exercise also reminded Cleo of the ranch: <u>everyone is being asked to do more with less.</u> As both teams applied themselves, Cleo and

Napoleon crept closer in hopes of getting a glance at these engineering masterpieces–both horses were blessed with keen eyesight.

When they saw the drawings, both Cleo and Napoleon tried hard to restrain themselves because the crafts looked so ridiculous. Cleo placed a bet with Napoleon that the green team had one chance in three of succeeding and that the red team had one chance in five. The discussion among team members was lively as the 30-minute planning phase came to an end. The teams were obviously anxious to get on with the actual construction process.

As the next phase began, Napoleon commented, "I hope their building skills are better than their drawing skills."

Cleo replied, "I wonder if they have done enough planning and thinking; all too often around the ranch, I see animals doing work before they have thought things through."

Napoleon concurred. "We certainly won't meet Mr. Mossback's production requirements the way things are going. I bet that we could save the ranch 25% by doing things right the first time. I really don't think most of the animals understand what it costs to run this place and how stiff the competition is. You know this country is consuming more and more imported beef, lamb, and wheat."

Cleo's reaction was typical for a work horse, "I see old Mossback taking off for vacations all the time, and what about that new four-wheel-drive truck he is driving? You can't tell me we are not profitable and that our unit costs are out of line. I didn't come out here to argue with you about our profit and loss statement. Let's relax and enjoy the excitement. Besides, if we are lucky, we will be in for some good laughs when they <u>deep six</u> these rafts in the pond."

As Cleo and Napoleon looked on, the excitement was building. For some reason, the teams seemed to be trying to outpace each other. Cleo and Napoleon couldn't figure it out. Nobody had declared this a race, or a competition with a winner and a loser. The stated goal was simply to get people across the pond as safely as possible. Cleo and Napoleon couldn't understand why the two teams were accusing each other of espionage and getting angry. The red team was clearly moving faster when one of the red team members secretly switched their original inner tube with the green team's inner tube.

Napoleon said, "It's obvious the red team started out with a smaller tube."

"That's cheating."

"You're right, Cleo. Why didn't they ask or see if parts could be interchangeable or if they could pump the inner tube up with more air."

"They want to WIN! You have a lot to learn. Humans have big egos, so they have to prove that they are better, no matter what the cost."

Cleo was amazed by how devious and brutal these teams had become with each other. Napoleon suspected that things would only get more interesting as the drama continued to unfold.

Whether Napoleon had telepathic abilities or not, more organization debacles and team dysfunctions were in the offing. As the humans completed the construction of their amazing floating machines, the organizers of this spectacle brought all of the activities to a halt. This seemed curious to Cleo and Napoleon, who couldn't wait for the rafts to hit the water. They hadn't had a good laugh for weeks and were doing their best to restrain themselves.

Then it started–wailing and gnashing of teeth that could be heard across the entire ranch. The red and green teams were furious. It had all happened rather fast. After the humans gathered around the organizer, the only thing she did was to distribute the following memo to each team:

> *In real organization situations, it often becomes necessary to respond and adapt to changes and demands. The implications of these new challenges are not always met with enthusiasm. However, the true test of any team is its ability to respond to problems and bring about changes that are not easily accomplished. Consequently, we want to inform you that the red and green teams must now exchange rafts and proceed on with their respective missions.*

The resulting cries were resounding and vivid. "You can't do this to us." "We refuse." "How can we trust their piece of junk; no way will that float." "You are doing exactly what headquarters does to us out in the field ... dictates, mandates, and edicts." "Why did you wait and tell us now?"

Cleo and Napoleon were flabbergasted. From their perspective, neither raft would pass EPA, OSHA, DOT, or Coast Guard Standards for a sea-worthy or "pond"-worthy vessel. They couldn't see why either team would argue or degrade the other team's work. The level of **resistance** about the prospect of having to change in midstream was appalling. Each team member seemed to have contributed to and "owned" their team's craft–they were attached.

Cleo said, "I have never seen a group of crybabies like this before. Why can't they cooperate and go on with the task? How can they possibly tell which raft will work better?"

As the two mighty horses watched the spectacle in utter amazement, they couldn't help but reflect back to some events that had occurred on the ranch just the previous week. Mossback had purchased a new and lighter harness for Cleo that was supposed to make her work easier. Well, Cleo had kicked up a fuss and refused to work the entire day. Cleo didn't like the looks of the new harness and she felt like she had been forced to adopt another's idea. The week before that, a new lock had been put on the hen house because a fox had been spotted earlier by a fellow rancher. But the hens felt it was a bad idea. They trusted the old lock and assumed Mossback just wanted to keep them from running around too much. They believed the fox story was just a way to manipulate and scare them into liking the new lock. Then there was the day when it was announced that the milk truck driver would have to change his pick-up schedule. The cows were still fighting that change. The more Napoleon and Cleo thought about these events, the less bizarre the behavior of the humans became.

Napoleon said, "At first I was amazed at how hard the humans were fighting a simple change."

"I agree," said Cleo, "but now it seems clear that any time someone has a new idea, any time we have to make a change, we end up killing ourselves arguing and complaining."

The more the two talked, the clearer it became that whenever changes were introduced, everyone seemed to resist and fight. Often the problem seemed to be the way that change was introduced. Sometimes it seemed like the attitudes and perspectives of those affected by the change were preventing progress, creativity, and the pursuit of improvement. Could it be that the animals felt unappreciated because they hadn't been consulted and no one would even listen to their point of view?

Returning to the raft operation, everyone seemed unhappy with the turn of events. Neither the green nor the red team could rally enough energy and motivation to really carry on and launch their crafts. All of their anger was directed toward the organizer who had introduced the change. The humans were not in a humorous mood.

The organizer finally said,

> *"Look, the choice is yours. You have 30 more minutes. You can try to work and sail with the resources you now have, or you can throw in the towel. I encourage you to continue, but you have to make the final choice."*

"I like the way she said that," commented Napoleon. "She was right on the money–very direct and straightforward. After all, if they have to operate the raft, they should be able to make the final decision."

The most amazing thing happened next. Both teams begrudgingly approached the vessels they had so sadly inherited. The red team was still especially vocal about the inadequacies of its lot in life. The members appealed to the organizer three more times to be permitted to make alterations in their craft. The organizer had a curious way of rewarding the red team: she instructed them to make the crossing first. That really made them furious, but they finally relented and accepted the challenge.

In a frustrated mood they set the raft in the water amidst constant badgering of the green team. Demeaning, and degrading comments were being made about the work that the green team had invested in their raft. The green team was quiet, but you could see that the humor had worn off and they were taking the comments personally. The green team felt bad, and now, even before the crossing was attempted by the red team, their initial pride had melted into doubt and embarrassment. They could only defend themselves with counter charges about the vessel they would soon inherit.

Carefully the red team took their places on the raft; very slowly, they inched toward their designated spots. At first, the raft rolled and pitched. Cleo and Napoleon were glued to the scene. They didn't know whether to laugh or to cheer. The humans were tense, and their faces were white. One of them said, "I don't know how to swim."

The organizer counseled,

> *"Trust your life jacket, your team, and the work of the green team."*

The last person was finally on board, and one of the drums shifted for a minute under the weight. People panicked.

The green team was quiet, but intense, as they observed this critical phase of boarding. If the raft was to tip, now would be the time. With everyone on board safely, the skipper yelled, "Now what do we do?"

The green team answered, "Fortunately, we planned for a paddle with the last unused board. Use it to get across."

Cleo looked at Napoleon and said, "The fool. What did he think the board was for?"

The green team handed out the last board to propel the red team across. The skipper of the green team smiled and said, "Now let me ask you. How did you envision getting the raft you built for us across? You used all the timber."

"Hands and feet," he replied.

"You expect us to stick our hands and feet in the icy pond and kick our way across? Thanks a lot, red team!"

Cleo and Napoleon watched both teams succeed in sailing across successfully, without incident–in spite of team member's amazement, doubt, and initial resistance. In fact, the red team came out with fewer wet feet and completed its mission quickly with the use of the paddle.

Once on the other side, the organizer asked everyone to circle up and talk about how groups resist change and progress. Listening to their discussion gave the horses a new understanding about the workings of the ranch and the fresh insight that resistance to change is a widespread phenomenon. Knowing that Mr. Mossback usually set out fresh oats at 11:00 a.m., both horses hurried back to share their observations and perceptions with the rest of the animals.

# 9

To:      All Animals

From:   Cleo & Napolean

Subject: Resistance To
          Change Meeting

After their snack, Cleo and Napoleon convened an all animals meeting under the big elm tree. Even Mr. Mossback's labrador retriever, Guido, attended. The animals were astir to learn what had transpired down at the pond.

Cleo began, "You wouldn't believe what we saw–two groups of people building rafts to float across the pond. What was most amazing was that the teams spent their time arguing and fighting between themselves because each team had to float across on the raft built by the other team. After listening to the humans talk about what happened, Napoleon and I have some ideas for changes we might like to make here on the ranch."

Guido asked, "Napoleon, you travel around with Mr. Mossback. Are humans like this all the time?"

"If you mean set in their ways, that's hard to answer," responded Napoleon. "After watching and listening to these two groups, I do believe that humans feel strongly about preserving the status quo."

The rooster, prancing around, said, "Just as I thought, inflexible."

"I think it is more subtle than that," Napoleon countered. "Each team developed 'ownership' in its raft–the team members were comfortable with what they had constructed, and each team wanted to achieve its goal. When they were instructed to change to the other team's raft, each team perceived a risk which triggered a resistance. It seems to me the issue is maintaining the status quo versus taking a risk."

Cleo, pawing the ground for attention, said, "The way I saw it, each team at the pond had faith in its own thinking process and the product the team members had developed. The raft symbolized security: they had built it, had confidence in their workmanship, and felt safe in it. Humans seem to be very concerned with self-preservation."

"Who isn't?" asked Guido.

Napoleon then said, "I have been thinking deeply about that, and I have a possible explanation for what Cleo and I saw.

Deep inside most of us are two competing forces or motivations: Number one is the drive or desire to achieve, succeed, live, experiment, and take appropriate risks and to experience change and variety in our lives. Number two is the drive or desire to be cautious and avoid losses, play it safe, go with the status quo, avoid exposure to risks, and protect our own importance.

You can see this yourself by watching the animals play or work here on the ranch. Sometimes we feel like taking a risk and living dangerously. Other times we prefer to curl up in our security straw blankets of life and hold back. It seems to me that the members of each team at the pond had developed their own human security blanket that was symbolized by the raft they had built and had confidence in. The difficulty with these two competing forces is that they are subtle. In other words, we can unconsciously and unintentionally drift back and forth between these two drives much like the almost imperceptible movement of the teeter-totter when the Mossback children try to bring it into balance. The movement is sometimes very gradual, perhaps noticeable only to those who are observing and not actually on the teeter-totter or wrapped up in the task or problem."

"Good point," snorted Short Ribs, the pig. We should be the last to forget that resistance and fears or hesitation caused by unknown challenges, risks, and threats are natural and healthy. But a preoccupation with avoiding risk would mean that none of us would ever venture out of the barnyard. It is okay to resist things that are not right, but the harsh reality of life is that you can't learn, grow, develop talents, and contribute to our team's mission without getting scraped up or hurt, without taking some chances and being made uncomfortable in the process."

Guido asked, "Do we agree then that resistance can be justified in some situations, that it sometimes serves a healthy and useful purpose, while in other situations, it is unhealthy and artificially blocks group or individual development, change, and evolution?" All the animals nodded in agreement.

Filling the silence, Napoleon said, "Yes, but deciding whether resistance is justified or unjustified can be slippery when you are personally involved, like in the boat-building situation. A clear conscious decision on whether to overcome resistance takes some objective introspection and reflection, as well as help from those who are unaffected by the threat or fear of change. It requires that we think long range versus short range, consider the situation from others' perspectives, and contemplate our true goals and values.

Earlier we talked about the teeter-totter and how it can move ever so gently, even undetectable to the individual or group on it. So it is with resistance, in that it can creep up like a fox in a hen house, so gradually that we can't detect any conscious or deliberate decisions on our part to resist a new course of action or a new program, a new leader or method of working."

Cleo responded, "I don't think the humans were aware that resistance had set in-it was such a natural response to a new course of action, not a deliberate decision on their part to resist. But even I could see that their actions-postponing, delaying, deferring, rechecking, analysis paralysis, etc.-were no longer productive, that the threat to the status quo had infected their perspective and distorted their view of reality."

"Infected is a good word to describe it," Napoleon responded. Catching the resistance virus is like catching any virus-you can't tell immediately or exactly where it came from. Like most viruses, resistance is hard to cure once it has affected or infected your thought process and attitude toward a problem or task.

Short Ribs snorted, "If you are so smart, just where does this resistance, hesitation, reluctance, or cautiousness come from?"

Napoleon proceeded, "I believe that the core or foundation of resistance is lodged deep in the bedrock of our needs and emotions. As individual animals or groups, we have a tremendous need to be safe, to be in control, to be free to choose and to avoid oppression, to win and succeed, to be competent, and to have the respect and admiration of others. When events occur that interfere with our freedom and power to choose, when we feel oppressed or challenged, or when our turf and sense of importance are threatened, we are capable of both conscious and subconscious types of resistance. The response may manifest itself in subtle indirect actions or direct and radical behaviors that show our resistance. When that core set of needs or desires is threatened by a real or perceived situation or when it appears that events are leading us beyond our threshold of tolerance for vulnerability, we act out a wide variety of different types of resistance. At first, it may not even be clear to us or others why we have embarked on a set of resistant actions or reactions. This behavior is observable after we have mentally processed the situation and either consciously or subconsciously identified a threat to our core needs. Our perception drives our interpretations and behavior.

If you will permit me, I think I can use my hoof to draw on the ground a picture of how resistance grows and develops through four stages." Napoleon proceeded to rough out the following diagram:

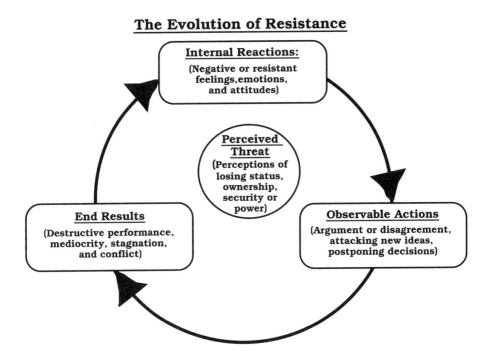

## The Evolution of Resistance

**Internal Reactions:**
(Negative or resistant feelings, emotions, and attitudes)

**Perceived Threat**
(Perceptions of losing status, ownership, security or power)

**End Results**
(Destructive performance, mediocrity, stagnation, and conflict)

**Observable Actions**
(Argument or disagreement, attacking new ideas, postponing decisions)

Guido, who had been extremely amazed by Napoleon's artistic abilities and attentive to his analysis of the situation, finally barked up, "I am interested as to how we can all get a grip on unintentional/subtle resistance since it is kind of hard to detect."

"Ah, now you are at the heart of what we have to consider," responded Napoleon. Coping with unintended, unconscious resistance is different from dealing with deliberate, intended, and strategically planned and orchestrated resistance. How do we recognize the difference and avoid succumbing to the security of maintaining the status quo?"

Cleo moved to the center of the group and said, "Fellow animals, I think we can learn from the humans' mistakes and still meet the needs that Napoleon has so clearly described."

"I am game for anything that will make our lives better," barked Guido. "When do you let us in on what you two learned from the humans? How did they decide to choose a productive course of action after they had perceived themselves as exposed and vulnerable?"

Napoleon said, "Cleo paid close attention to their discussion. It seemed to focus on how they could objectively process or reassess the situation and choose a productive course of action when the perception of threat was unjustified and shortsighted. Cleo, why don't you summarize what the two teams decided?"

Cleo, clearing the ground with her massive hoof, said, "They agreed as a team to follow nine rules:

1.   Understand that resistance is normal, and avoid the urge to attack, degrade, or put down those who are resisting.

2.  Offer constructive alternatives regarding ways to move on; after all, the resistance may be the result of some basic objections, legitimate differences, or very real threats. See if there are new "win-win" proposals or solutions, and test these out in the group.

3.  If this approach fails, understand that the resistance may be unintended, subconscious, or unplanned. In this case the resistance needs to be brought to the surface, confronted, named, described, and set out for examination in a neutral, non-threatening way. When you see a group caught in the resistance cycle, floundering and chasing their tails, someone has to assume responsibility and muster up the courage to start the "truth process."

"Truth process?" barked Guido, "I don't understand."

Napoleon interrupted, "What is necessary is stating the obvious in accurate but gentle and non-provocative terms. It is too harsh to say, 'I think you are all afraid of trying something new,' or 'You are all talk and no action.' This approach will only invite more defensiveness and resistance–the self-discovery process is blocked. The humans agreed that the more effective approach was to say, 'We have analyzed this problem four times and need to consider some solutions,' or 'This is the third time we have delayed a decision, what issues are blocking our progress?' If we can adopt a similar approach, we will all be more likely to look in the mirror and reassess what is happening."

"That seems simple enough," snorted Short Ribs. "Can't the humans do that?"

"Sounds easy, but they all agreed to follow some additional rules," added Cleo.

4.  Be patient. Even when resistance is approached positively, prepare yourself for some denial, defensiveness, or blaming—it is not easy for individuals to let go of their perceptions. Be prepared to identify and describe the resistance more than once and from a variety of angles.

5.  Give the group time and space to internalize and absorb the message. Don't move too quickly in making suggestions, overselling techniques, or compromising courses of action. Repackaging, selling, or compromising won't cut through resistance.

Short Ribs then spoke up, "I think silence is the most underutilized communication tool here on the ranch. All too often we succumb to the opposing principle: The loudest mouth takes the lead."

"Good point," responded Cleo. "We saw plenty of that from the humans. Here is the next rule they created:

6.  Be compassionate, and offer some support and encouragement. The team may need a dose of hope and optimism to face the needed change and new ways of thinking and acting."

Napoleon added, "Humans often feel some grief and pain in letting go and moving on. Patience, compassion, and support were felt to be of great importance by the teams. These helped each team deal with the harsh reality of adopting a new position or way of thinking."

"They also agreed to follow three more rules," added Cleo.

7.  Explore choices with consideration of everyone's feelings, and reinforce the point that resistance is a choice, just as moving beyond resistance is a choice.

"You'll like the word these humans used to illustrate this, Short Ribs–wallow," added Napoleon.

"As a team, they agreed that what they need to do is help bring light and clarity to their choices. They don't want to be denied their rights to stay bogged down in resistance. Sometimes humans are not ready to be pulled out of a situation, and they need to 'wallow' and experience more pain, discomfort, and tension before they are motivated to act."

"When I wallow, I don't feel pain," snorted Short Ribs. "Humans are really strange!"

Guido barked, "It sounds like everyone needs to be open about sharing information and to trust each other. It also sounds like the teams need a clearly defined vision, goal, or destiny to guide them through the rough resistance stages."

"Exactly," Cleo went on. "Here are the last two rules they agreed to:

8.  Mutually agree on a vision, operating plans, responsibilities, individual commitments, and to focus on—future positive consequences and payoffs.

9.  Even if the team is only willing to think about overcoming its resistance, recognize this as a positive first step and celebrate. Even 'baby steps' in the right direction are an accomplishment. Getting started is half the battle."

Napoleon said, "It seems to me that if you sense that the level of readiness is high and a heightened level of awareness has been achieved, then you can draw up a specific action plan. It can be a collaborative effort by drawing out ideas and encouraging involvement from everyone."

Short Ribs jumped in, "You know, that is so true. It has always been amazing what we can accomplish as a team when no one cares who gets the credit."

Much discussion then ensued among the animals. Guido noticed Mr. Mossback walking toward the group and suggested, "The horses have given us much to think about. Since our meeting is about to be interrupted, I suggest we table our discussion until after dinner. But I, for one, think we can improve our situation on the ranch if we adopt a similar set of rules."

Napoleon and Cleo both whinnied and said in unison, "We do too, but just as we observed with the humans, it won't be easy to live by these rules when the next change affects us personally. May the lessons be with you."

Mr. Mossback called, "Cleo, come on, girl, time to harness up."

The animals dispersed, each looking forward to the discussion and vote that evening. Throughout the day, whenever two or more of the animals got together, the topic of conversation was how "intelligent" humans could get themselves in such a mess. Life on the ranch could never be like that.

# 10
## ORIENTEERING FOR PROFIT AND FUN

Most of the twenty-three other people I have shared the last three days with seem to be pretty relaxed after just completing another wonderful dinner. Diet city next week for me. Rumors floated around the dinner table about a long day tomorrow followed by a sleep out. As usual our consultants were vague when asked what we would be doing. Wait a minute, one of the consultants just handed Marvin a piece of paper, a compass, and a map. She put on the board the following message:

> *Departure time is at 6:30 a.m.–Plan on returning no sooner than 10:00 a.m. on the following day. Use your time tonight as you see fit.*

The consultant has left us alone. The group immediately huddles around Marvin who reads these instructions:

## THE CHALLENGE

You are about to undertake a journey that could lead to increased profits and organizational effectiveness. At stake is the very existence of your company. To succeed, you will need to employ all resources available–to come up short is to fall victim to the Spineless Price Cutters. Your goal is to obtain additional capital of

$280,000. Traveling with you are consultants who can be of value to you, should you care to purchase assistance from them.

You may approach the challenge any way you wish within a few general guidelines:

- No marker may be counted more than once.
- The minimum number of team players in any one group is four.
- In order to achieve the point, all members of the team must be within 20 feet of it.
- The entire group (24) must be at base camp by 1:30 p.m. You will be penalized $5,000 per minute for every minute you are late.
- It is important that you organize yourselves in a fashion that maximizes all resources and expertise.
- There will be a 45-minute audit performed by your consultant sometime during the course.

At various spots on your map are orienteering markers, each containing a black code letter and each worth a certain amount of money. You must use your map and compass, as well as some ingenuity and creativity, to find these markers. A bonus of $20,000 will be given if twenty of the potential twenty-four markers are collected. Your consultant also has the authority to award additional bonuses or penalties.

The route is quite challenging, including numerous hills that will excite the relatively experienced mountaineer. There will be ample opportunities for solitude, as well as sheer frenzy and the unexpected surprises of the great outdoors. We call this journey the "Trail of Tears".

Good Luck!"

# THE TEAM

Twenty-four leaders have spent the last three days in adventure-based management training designed to teach teamwork and leadership. Not once during these three days have they been asked to function as an entire twenty-four-person team. All they have to rely on is their own abilities and things they have learned by working as individuals or as members of either a six or twelve-person team over the past three days.

# THE DRAMA UNFOLDS

At first everyone is talking, either about the challenge, map, or compass. Then Amelia yells, "Wait a minute, we've pretty well seen over the last three days that unless we get organized and develop a well-thought-out plan we're not going to be able to pull this off. Now who has some ideas on how we can get organized?" Another person asks, "Has anyone ever done this before?" Three hands go up, and the group ask for each to tell about his/her experience. Two people had done some basic compass and map work as Explorer Scouts, but this was many years ago. The other person, Steve, is still in the Navy Reserves and works with a somewhat similar type of problem every summer when he fulfills his commitment to the Navy.

One member of the team says, "O.K. That's the experience we've got to work with; let's get going." A couple members of the group voice their agreement, but Steve says, "I'm as anxious as you to get going, but I think we need to figure out a way we can operate that will make everyone comfortable with our approach. I, for one, am not for charging forward on this half–cocked. My suggestion is that we break into our six-person groups. Each group will spend the next hour brainstorming ideas on both the type of organization structure we need to be successful and how we can best accomplish our mission as an entire team." A few members ask for clarification on what each six-person group is to do, but the entire team agrees with this first step.

One hour later, each six-person group presents their ideas to the other team members. Each group has considered some different aspects of the challenge: the use of resources, team-member strengths and weaknesses, contingency plans, worst-case scenarios, methods of keeping in touch with other groups, etc. One similarity was the desire to divide the work so that each of the six-person groups could remain together.

One group presents a strong case for a central coordination group that will keep in contact with each group throughout the day via the portable radios that the consultants always keep with them. The team agrees with this idea and elects Steve to be the Chief Executive Officer(CEO) of the project and David, the Chief Financial Officer(CFO). These two will not actually go out on the course, but will remain at base camp to coordinate and communicate with the other groups. They will be responsible for monitoring the team progress and making any modifications to the original plan as conditions change throughout the day.

At this point Steve takes control of the meeting and suggests a break during which he will meet with a representative from each of the four groups. Steve states that since all twenty-four team members were leaders, the representatives from the groups should consider themselves as a "facilitator" of each group as opposed to its "leader." Their task is to develop and share different approaches for developing the plan of attack with the entire group.

After the break, Steve indicates that the six of them (CEO, CFO, and four group facilitators) are in agreement that members of each of the four groups should meet for half an hour and, based on the group's physical strengths and weaknesses, determine which points on the course they feel they can achieve and which they would rather have another group achieve. Additionally, they are to define and assign different roles to each person in the group. Mary, one of the four team facilitators, suggests these roles: back-up facilitator, map reader, navigator, and a pacer to monitor the progress and physical capabilities of the group members.

One-half-hour later, members of each of the four groups report that they are ready for tomorrow, and they review which of the twenty-four points their group is willing to go after, based on their physical abilities. Each group also has adopted a name for itself: Alpha, Bushwackers, Six Pack, and Range Riders.

After each group has given its report, Evelyn, one of the team members, suggests they wait until tomorrow to make actual point assignments since more than one group is willing to assume responsibility for some of the twenty-four points. Her logic is that once everyone sees the actual terrain and start point, the map may take on a different look. Everyone is in agreement, and one person suggests the entire team talk about an ideal scenario and a number of worst-case scenarios. There is widespread suspicion that the consultants will have a few surprises for each group once they are out on the course. The next hour is spent planning for a number of "what if" situations and establishing check-in times of 9:00, 10:30, and 12:00.

Consultants observing the whole process comment that the team's commitment and energy grew the more they talked. Everyone has a clear picture of the day and possible contingencies. The team meeting ends with a number of cheers and shouts as twenty-four tired individuals head for a long-awaited sleep.

## MEETING THE CHALLENGE

At 6:30 a.m. the team climbs on the bus for a 30-minute ride into a very desolate location surrounded by deep ravines and hills with an elevation of 7,000 feet. The last 8 miles are on a winding dirt road. The topographic map that each member has covers only about 5 square miles. As the bus proceeds, each person is anxiously trying to place their exact location on this limited map. When the bus stops, various guesses are made as to their present location.

The CEO states that the four group facilitators and CFO will meet and agree on which points each group will be assigned. The individual groups will then meet to determine the route or sequence order to use in capturing these assigned points. The other team members get off the bus and anxiously look over their surroundings, trying to verify for themselves just where they are on the maps they have been given. Twenty minutes later, the entire team is ready to start. Each group has its assignments, and the CEO and CFO have recorded the specific route each group will follow. After a quick review by the CEO of the check-in times and contingency plan for the worst-case scenario (the four groups will be totally cut off from each other), the four separate groups depart.

The CEO and CFO stay at the base camp, or command central as they call it, with one consultant. At 8:55 a.m., 5 minutes before the agreed-to check-in time, the CEO asks the consultant to explain how the radio works so he can contact the four groups. The consultant states that safety dictated that all available radios be out on the course, and she has none to offer the CEO and CFO. A basic assumption that they will be able to maintain radio contact is false; the four groups are cut off from command central.

The CEO and CFO quickly meet. They discuss the merits of sitting and doing nothing for the next four hours or trying to vector into another team and thus avail themselves a radio. After a review of the map and routes that each team is following, they decide to stay together and take a straight line path to Alpha group's third point. With compass and map, the CEO and CFO plot an intercept course with Alpha group. After forty-five minutes, with much climbing and walking, the CEO and CFO find Alpha group's third point in a tall stand of aspen on the down side of a hill. But the Alpha group is not in sight.

The CEO and CFO express their confidence in each group and belief that they will stick to the predetermined plan. They also recognize that the groups do not really need them since the commitment of individual members to the plan is what is driving each group now. Their dilemma is whether to wait for Alpha group on the assumption that they have not visited this point or backtrack to Alpha group's second point. Since they have already become active, they decide to backtrack to Alpha group's second point, hoping to meet them along the way. About twenty minutes later, CFO spots a group about 1 mile away, just cresting an opposing hill. Using whistles and the sun's reflections off of a pocket knife, they are able to get the other group's attention. After a series of shouts, they determine that this is the Alpha group heading toward their third point. The current facilitator for the Alpha group yells that they will come to the CEO and CFO.

The CEO and CFO sit down for a traverse that could take upwards of 45 minutes considering the rough terrain separating them from the Alpha group. The CEO states that when they meet he will confer privately with the group's facilitator to find out their status, as well as information from other groups, and to express their dilemma. He also recommends that he should not take over the group but let the current facilitator maintain his or her position, with the CEO and CFO present only to provide support and make recommendations. They both agree that this will be the best approach.

As Alpha group approaches, CEO notices that the facilitator who was in charge at the start of the day is blindfolded and that another member seems to be hurt because she needs the assistance of two other group members. When they meet, the current facilitator explains that a freak, but fictitious, landslide caused the facilitator to lose his eyesight and one other member to break her leg. The total group has been proceeding at a much slower pace, missed their second point, and were trying to go for their fourth point and then circle back for points three and two since they were on the way back to base camp.

The CEO states that they have been to the group's third point and believe they are on a straight course to their second point. Since a point cannot be claimed with fewer than four people, he suggests they join forces and go to the third point, which is a quarter mile from the road. Once there, they can send the blind and injured persons to the road where they can easily travel back to the base camp, while the remainder of the group goes to the second and fourth point and back to base camp. The total group holds a lengthy discussion and agrees not to split any members off from the group. Everyone wants to be involved, even if they cannot see or walk as fast as the others. They agree and move out to the group's third point.

As they walk, the CFO reviews all the information the group's facilitator had as of 10:30 a.m. when the four groups had a conference call. On the basis of this information, he recommends to the CEO that they not have any more telephone contact with the other groups until 12:30 p.m. The CEO agrees and telephones a general message to the other three groups: "We're doing great. Believe in the plan and work the plan. Only use the telephone in case of emergency. We will have one final contact at 12:30 p.m. to see if we need to off-load any points on other groups that have finished early."

After they reach the third point the consultant calls for an audit (read debrief of the exercise up to the present) and leads a discussion of the progress, roles, and processes the group has been using throughout the day. The discussion centers on those factors both within and between the teams that are contributing to their apparent success. On the positive side, these points are discussed:

- We are sticking to our plan.
- Everyone has played an active role so far.
- When we have faced a challenge, like our navigator losing her speech and sight, we have all been involved in solving the problem.
- The group feels good about how they are progressing.

On the negative side, these points are discussed:

- We still don't seem to listen to everyone.
- When we place a female in the facilitator role, the males seem to patronize her.
- We need to be more concerned about our team and not just about collecting a point.
- We aren't stretching ourselves to see where and how we can improve as a team.

At the end of the audit time, the consultant states that before the group proceeds to their second and final point, everyone except Amelia is muted. Since Amelia has not been involved in any of the map or compass reading so far during the day and, in fact, has played a very passive role, this creates a new dilemma for the group to overcome.

After two aborted routes, the Alpha group straggles into their second point at 12:30 p.m. During the journey from point three to two, the need has arisen to resolve some conflict, anger, and questions of trust. As the group approaches point two, even the casual observer would have to agree that they look like a very tight-knit unit, with each member physically supporting the others. The journey has brought about a significant transformation for this group.

At point two, the CEO makes his last call and learns that the other three groups are on course and should make the start point a little ahead of the finish time. At 1:30 p.m. all four groups are back at the start point. All but two of the twenty-four points have been captured. Financially the team has earned $275,000 plus $60,000 in bonuses to separate groups for exceptional group performance. Other groups have cost the team $20,000 in penalties for poor group performance and telephone expenses of $15,000. The team has exceeded its objective.

# 11

# TEAM DEBRIEF OF ORIENTEERING

All twenty-four members are seated in a semicircle on the ground, relaxing and reliving the day. A consultant asks the CEO to lead the total team debrief of this exciting and successful day. The CEO starts by making a request that before they go over the financial figures, each group facilitator relate to the entire team his/her group's experiences during the day.

The facilitator of the Bushwacker group stands up and, with emotion, asks that the other four members of the group, plus the CFO, join him to help in their group's review. The six, four men and two women, stand before the total team in a line, with arms around the shoulders or waists of the persons next to them. It is worth noting that the Bushwackers were assigned the highest, roughest terrain and most physically challenging points. The facilitator says he would like to start and then let each member add his/her own personal comments. "We decided that the journey would be a chance for each of us to experience the role of facilitator and get feedback from the others on what we did which was helpful or harmful to the group. Therefore, we rotated this role, with a new person assuming this responsibility at each point. We also agreed that our journey and how we operated as a team during this journey was more important than successfully getting all our points. Our feeling was that if we got our points at the expense of our team we would have lost, so we kept the health and well-being of each individual and of the team as a whole at the forefront. The CFO was a member of our group, even though he stayed at command central. We want him to know that we appreciate his sacrifice and that he was with us all the way. I would now like each of the other members to add their perspective, and I can fill in on anything they overlook."

Here are direct quotes from the members of the Bushwacker group about what they experienced, learned, and will take away from this day:

"When I was the facilitator, members of my group trusted me and allowed me to fail. I didn't know how to read a map or compass, but they were very supportive and forced me to take the responsibility."

"We trusted each other."

"I was the slowest, but the group didn't make this difference a big deal; in fact, they accommodated me and didn't make me feel bad."

"We each helped one another develop the skills to get the job done. In the end, anyone could have done anybody's job."

"There was real deep caring for one another. We adjusted our speed, asked for help, and received support."

"I learned to respect each person's strengths as different from my own and how to subordinate my individual needs to those of the group."

"I felt we were more than a group. It might sound corny, but I think we really exhibited a sense of community and caring."

"We accomplished our goal because each of us learned how to give up our selfish needs and be concerned with the group's efforts."

"We cared enough to be honest with one another during our debriefs. As a result, people changed and the group was more effective."

"I learned that I could have more influence with the group if I let go of the power I thought I had when I was a facilitator."

"People in my group allowed me to stretch and grow today, and it felt good."

"There wasn't a curve ball the consultants could throw at us. We were flexible and knew how to work together to get any job done."

After listening to these comments the consultant says there is only one thing he can add, "This group of people are the greatest."

The other three groups gave similar reports and reactions. The CEO and CFO then end with the financial figures, and the consultants say it is time to load up and head for base camp. The team doesn't really make any moves to get on the bus. It is as if they want to savor the moment and fear that the magic of the day, teamwork, will not get on the bus with them. After much encouragement from the consultants, the bus is finally loaded and off.

The team reconvenes for dinner that night. On the blackboard in the room someone has written:

**"We came here as 24 individuals. We now are one unbeatable community"**

**—anon.**

## CONSULTANT'S NOTE:

Having observed over fifty teams performing this exercise, the team reported here has been the most effective and inspiring. I am glad to have had a ringside seat to watch successful teamwork in action.

# 12

# In Search Of Team Member Alignment— A Leadership Fable

Once in an organization called LEXON, there was a very successful team leader. Her team always exceeded their goals; and she found joy in working with such energetic, committed, and caring people. When a job came open in her group, a lot of people chose to apply. Some were even willing to take a pay cut to "have some fun again at work". Those who accepted career opportunities and went off to manage their own teams always left with a feeling of sadness and the promise to do their best at building teams that were just as effective. Some managers in the organization were actually envious of this leader and her team, but even the most political in-fighter had to admit that there was indeed magic in the group.

As you may have guessed, this team had not always been so effective and successful. The leader could remember many years when, despite their struggles, they did no better than other groups. The straw that broke the camel's back was the strategic planning meeting. What a frustrating fiasco! How could eight apparently rational adults spend so much time and get so little done? The constant disagreement and jockeying for position meant that no one person or small faction was able to make any progress. It just didn't make sense to the leader how a group of people employed in the same department could work so ineffectively together and be so disrespectful of one another. What was even worse was that the complaints from customers had been increasing, and no one, but herself was particularly disturbed.

Thinking about the old days she smiled, recalling how glad she was that she had discovered the key to teamwork–and, more importantly, that she had put it to use. She looked forward to and enjoyed team meetings and the other opportunities they had to work together as a group, something that many of her peers could not understand. For them teamwork was a necessary evil, not the positive experience they had heard her speak of with such conviction.

But, back to our story. Things had not always been such fun. There was a time when she had almost asked to go back to being an individual contributor. She was sure that management wasn't for her, especially after that dreadful strategic meeting. Later that evening, in her aerobic class, while running in place to the sound of Michael Jackson's "Beat It," she wondered:

> Is management for me?
> What do I really want from a career?
> Why do I let these meetings upset me?
> Why do I care? They are just employees.
> How important is this anyway?
> What is my commitment?

*"So just beat it . . . just beat it . . . "*

"You're right, Michael," she yelled, "I'm not going to quit! No decisions until I learn what teamwork takes!" With that she ran toward the showers, with the resolve to start the next morning in her search for some answers.

# THE SEARCH

She called a management professor at the local community college and some of her friends in management positions both within her company and at others in the metro area. More than one mentioned that they had attended seminars on building teamwork conducted by Mr. Martinovich, a very successful plant manager. With further investigation she found that not only did this manager talk about building teams, he had on more than one occasion turned entire plants around by using his team concepts. She decided to set up an appointment with Mr. Martinovich.

# THE DISCUSSION

At nine o'clock the next morning, she went through an office door marked with the name plate, Alex Ivan Martinovich (AIM). "I am glad you could find time to meet with me, Mr. Martinovich," she began.

"Please call me AIM; with a name like mine, people have found my nickname much easier. From the tone of your voice and our brief discussion, I think I know just what you'd like to talk about."

"Did I sound that desperate?"

"No," replied AIM. "You sounded like a person who has taken the traditional approaches to teamwork about as far as they can go and who is still not happy with the results."

"I take it this is not the first time you have had this type of discussion."

"That's right. And, like the others before you, you sounded like you were open and ready to learn. That's why I agreed to meet with you."

Perhaps some of you are wondering what Alex Ivan Martinovich (AIM) was like, and some of you may already be casting him in the hero's role. Maybe so, I will let you make up your mind on that. Suffice it to say, he had a reputation of being able to turn organizations around and to do so with the willing cooperation of the employees. This reputation had given him the opportunity to work with hostile unions and within badly neglected facilities. Having tested and modified his opinion for thirty years, he was sure of what it takes to successfully turn an organization around.

You might ask, "What was he still doing in a plant manager's job?" AIM would have told you that he had a real liking for the people who have to get dirty to get their jobs done and that an office on the twentieth floor, surrounded by pinstripes, was not his idea of fun. Make no mistake–the opportunities and offers had been there–he had made a choice not to pursue them.

Our team leader is getting impatient, so I had better continue the story. Looking around the office, she noticed a tarnished plaque on the wall which read:

*Visions produce greatness—Always AIM high!*

"Where did you get that?" she asked.

"My first work group presented that to me at a going-away party, when I changed companies."

"Your work group?" You see, she always thought visions were only for CEO's or other top managers, not for plant managers.

AIM asked if she minded if he smoked. She nodded no, so, lighting his pipe, he said, "I take it you and your team have not defined your vision?"

"We can't even agree on our strategic plan. That is what prompted me to call you."

"I would suggest that your strategy is dependent upon your vision. Without that, is it any wonder your group can't agree on how to get there?" asked AIM.

"I have already told you our team leader doesn't think visions are important for a middle-level manager and team. Are they?"

"You must decide that for yourself, after you have heard me to the end."

Before she could respond, AIM handed her this wallet–sized card:

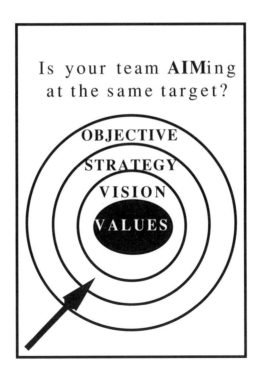

"I keep this card in my wallet to remind me that the team's vision is an expression of the values we want to see enacted in our work environment. The vision is a relatively stable foundation for our strategy and objectives. Strategy communicates what we are in business to accomplish; some people also call it mission. Our objectives are both team and individually based, and they outline what we specifically want to accomplish this year. This target helps remind us that our integrity as a team should be judged by the consistency between our values, vision, strategy, and objectives."

Lest you think that AIM was taking a theoretical sidetrack, he asked, "What is your team trying to invent?"

She responded quickly, "We're not in the business of inventing; we're in the business of doing."

"Let me ask another question," he said. "How will your department be different because you and the people have worked there?" Or, "What makes your department different from every other department in your company, or from a similar department in other companies—What is your dream?"

She couldn't answer.

If you, like our team leader, think it is O.K. not to articulate your team's dream or aspirations, your team is not all it could be. But that is another story.

After an agonizing period of silence, AIM just started talking. "How do you expect your group to get excited about or committed to working as a team when they don't even know the type of collective future they are trying to create?"

She truly couldn't see anything for the team to get excited about except their paychecks, and since they were based on individual performance, no wonder the teamwork was so sloppy... "Are you saying we need to define the vision for our department, our team?"

By golly, I think she's got it.

Repacking his pipe, AIM just nodded his agreement, adding, "Without a vision to help navigate your actions, your team will drift and be exposed to the currents and winds of fate."

Some of you, like our team leader, may be wondering what is involved in a vision. For the benefit of our team leader, let me quote from a speech AIM presented at the last Chamber of Commerce meeting:

> "Is your unit great? Not your company, your work unit–your team. I would bet against it and win far more than I would lose–any takers? Just as I thought.
>
> If your team is not great or actively striving for greatness, as a leader you have failed. Here is another proposition: I would be willing to bet that members of your unit cannot articulate the team's collective vision–any takers?
>
> Is this because of domestic or foreign competition, untrained workers, the bureaucracy, inferior supplies, organized labor, or governmental interference? No, it's because of what we as leaders haven't done–we're both the problem and the solution.
>
> Before you vote to rescind my membership, I decided to get you upset because the message I have is important to our collective competitiveness: We will continue to fail until

leaders and their teams, at all levels of the organization, recognize the need to define and articulate their vision. What, you might ask, is a vision? I don't know if I have all the answers, but I believe a good vision is compelling and addresses the future. Specifically it defines six parameters:

- What greatness is for this team
- How they want their values to be lived out in their unit
- What the unit has to offer that will truly make a difference
- How they are going to manage their business to achieve their wants, wishes, and dreams for the future
- How their customers and clients should be treated
- How they should treat each other

Lest you think that I have been smoking some strange cigarettes, here are some sample statements from teams that I have been associated with:

- We will encourage every team member to take risks, make decisions, exercise initiative, and never be afraid to make mistakes.
- We will act as partners with our customers and clients.
- We will treat every person with whom we come in contact with respect and dignity.
- We will recognize achievement and celebrate success.
- We will have only one class of team member—each member will be a full partner.
- We will not tolerate anyone who looks down on others.
- We will not tolerate anyone who tries to move ahead at the expense of others.

- And, finally, we will all have fun participating in a great adventure—building our department."

Our team leader responded in wonderment, "I believe in most of those things."

AIM didn't have the heart to tell her that we all have a vision; the problem is we keep it in the closet. For groups to work as teams, the members must be aligned with the vision. Thus, the key is for the team collectively to articulate who they are and what they stand for.

Instead, AIM just nodded, "I thought you did; that is why I agreed to have this meeting with you. This type of thinking goes beyond traditional management wisdom."

"I think I will schedule an off-site meeting with my team to define our vision. AIM, you have been very helpful."

"I would like to hear how your meeting goes. Can we get together two months from today?" AIM asked.

Now let two months pass, all in a twinkling. One of the great things about tales is how fast time can pass. During these two months, the team has held three full-day meetings. You would know this was a fairy tale if I told you the meetings were easy—they weren't. Without a structured process to follow and a lot of trust and perseverance from everyone, the team would have bogged down.

Developing visions is hard work. It is not for those who have only surface commitment.

Since I have chosen to focus on the positive, let me return to the story. The team weathered the storm and reached consensus on what their vision should contain and what the exact wording of it would be. Our team leader now sits in AIM's office beaming from ear to ear.

If you had asked AIM to predict the results of the meetings, he could have, with a high probability of success. Rather than rob our team leader of the opportunity to affirm her team's accomplishments, he just asked her, "How did it go?"

Like the popping of a champagne cork, her story bubbled out. She noted that it was tough at first, with more than one of the team members skeptical. But, after they saw how serious she was, they started to come around. There is a lot of detail we won't go into here. Suffice it to say, she felt the team became very unified behind a common cause.

Does this mean there wouldn't be differences or conflicts within the team? Absolutely not—in fact, she hoped not, because these are the basis for creativity. What she was sure of was that the team could handle these differences and conflicts in an open and honest fashion.

She concluded her story noting that the atmosphere at work had changed and people seemed to welcome working together. She certainly enjoyed being their manager and couldn't think of doing anything else as challenging and rewarding.

AIM smiled. "What amazes me is you haven't once mentioned what your team's vision statement says."

You probably think that after three long meetings the thing she would be the proudest of is the final product, the vision statement.

Our team leader evidenced a great deal of insight when she said, "What I discovered along the way is that the heart of a vision is not so much the actual words, but the act of creating it and then making a commitment to carry it out. I will leave you a copy to study at your leisure. What I wanted to do today was share my excitement over the process we went through and our transformation from a collection of individuals to a team."

"Splendid," replied AIM, "you have captured the magic so poignantly; do you mind if I use that in my next speech?"

"Not at all. It's the least I can do."

"Can I make one final observation?" asked AIM.

"Of course."

"We started this discussion because of your frustration during the strategic planning meeting. I believe your team is now ready to tackle the development of strategy, tactics, and goals for the coming year. My observation to keep in mind is this: you and the team's integrity will be evaluated by how consistent your day-to-day actions—in other words, strategies, tactics, and goals—are with the values outlined in your vision statement."

Our team leader just smiled and said, "Thank you very much. You have given me much to think about."

Relighting his pipe, AIM responded, "That is a value I cherish."

# 13

# SHARED LEADERSHIP— WHO'S THE LEADER?

Remember when you were a child, participating with the neighborhood kids in an informal game of basketball, soccer, football, or volleyball? It was fun, and everyone took part in determining who was to play what position, when, and for how long. Whether your team was winning or losing, everyone had the right to express ideas on needed changes. No one person had the authority to make decisions, yet some had more influence on the team than others.

What is the difference between those neighborhood teams that played children's games and a team of employees striving to accomplish a common goal? In the effective teams we have observed, the approach is the same whether they are meeting outdoor challenges like those described in this book or working on real tasks. For the ineffective teams, the differences are dramatic.

The most important difference is who assumes the responsibility for leadership. In the case of ineffective teams, the appointed manager universally emerges as the team leader. In effective teams, the responsibility for leadership is shared by all team members including the manager.

**Shared leadership** is the willingness to take charge when the need arises. It exists when the team is willing to allow many people the opportunity to influence the direction or approach the team will take. Shared leadership is a choice that every team member makes–to depend on the appointed leader, or to attempt to influence the team and accept leadership responsibility. Why is leadership shared in some teams and not in others? At least three forces are at work:

## 1. FORCES WITHIN THE ORGANIZATION

Formal organizations tend to suppress individual creativity, judgment, and energy. Bureaucracies sacrifice these characteristics for conformity, predictability, discipline, and a false sense of loyalty and security.

The elements that undergird this narrow view of organization include restrictive job descriptions, narrowly defined roles and responsibilities, rules, procedures, linear hierarchy, lack of cross training, and functional specialization. When pushed to the extreme, these principles of organization drive out anyone but the appointed manager from assuming leadership responsibilities— "That's what he gets paid the big bucks for–it's not my job."

## 2. FORCES WITHIN THE PERSON

When things are not going well, it is too easy of a cop-out to place all the blame on the organizations you work for. Leadership is an act of courage–to step out, advocate, assert yourself, and take a risk–you could be wrong. The ideal is team players who can assume a take-charge attitude when the need arises. Shared leadership becomes essential when the team is facing a problem, challenge, or adversity— not during periods of equilibrium, when the path ahead is smooth.

To choose to follow is safe. Leaders empower others to act, but first they must feel empowered themselves; empowered to question and test their assumptions, values, self-confidence, need for security, and self-imposed limits. Empowered to assert, to share their wisdom and inspiration. Leadership starts with a state of mind–to overcome the natural internal forces that keep individuals from taking the risks of stepping out, being vulnerable if wrong, and assuming responsibility.

## 3. FORCES WITHIN THE TEAM

Even when organizational policies, procedure, and climate foster individual initiative and people make the choice to assume leadership when the situation dictates, potential forces within the team can short-circuit these attempts:

**When team members are unwilling to defer, "dim their lights" and let others lead.** When the standard operating procedures are that you have to be number one and that promotions/recognition are at the expense of other team members, justifying this uncooperative behavior is easy. "If I can't lead, then I refuse to follow" is a fair description of this force.

**When a low level of trust and respect exists between team members.** Trust and respect are fragile and earned through genuine actions; without these qualities, attempts at influencing others will both be frustrating and foster a win-lose environment.

To illustrate the forces that may be present within the team and work against shared leadership, here is a composite list that we have heard too often during pre-training interviews with team members:

- We make fun of or belittle each other.
- There are too many cliques.

- People do things only based on a "What's in it for me?" attitude.
- Everyone wants to win alone. This creates a sick competition at the expense of cooperation.
- We have no cooperation on our team.
- Issues are taken to the manager instead of to the source.
- A lot of finger pointing goes on in this group.
- Public humiliation seems to be the norm.
- Everybody likes to be on top and look like the best member of the team.
- What we call communication is two people talking about a third person.
- Jealousy and a refusal to share ideas are key attributes of our team.
- Trust and respect are lacking.
- Cheating, lying, and taking credit as an individual for things that are accomplished by the team are common.
- Feelings of defensiveness are often exhibited.
- Gossiping is prevalent.
- Lack of personal responsibility characterizes our group.
- We don't talk about the team's real problems.
- We operate in a rigid atmosphere of intimidation—if you voice an opinion or try something new, you are subject to retribution.

Any combination of these forces will dissuade individual team members from venturing out to assume leadership during a given discussion. The antidote is for the team to recognize these destructive behaviors and create a strategy for bringing these perceptions/attitudes to light and dealing with them.

# LEADERSHIP STYLE —
# WHEN YOU HAVE NO POWER

The effectiveness of team members who attempt to assume leadership is dependent on their interpersonal communication styles. Acting like a leader doesn't guarantee that other team members will follow. Effective leadership requires someone to join the effort or cause that you are advocating. Your ability to influence others when you have no formal organizational power over them is enhanced if you keep the following approaches to interpersonal communication in mind when you advocate a change or want the team to deal with a problem:

- **Be descriptive, not accusing.** Statements or comments that are evaluative or judgmental tend to create a negative response in others. Describing what you see without a judgmental overtone is a more effective approach. A pointed question, "Why can't we reach a decision?" could cause other team members to defend their actions rather than talk about the real obstacles. A descriptive statement that might open the discussion is, "We have talked about this situation during three meetings without coming to closure."

- **Communicate a desire to collaborate in defining what you perceive as a mutual problem and in seeking a solution.** You want to let others know that you regard them as your equals and respect their ideas. After the problem is identified, room should be left for other team members to set their own goals, make their own decisions, and evaluate their own progress–or to collaborate with you in doing so.

- **Be empathic and supportive.** Team members have a stake in continuation of the status quo–recognize their feelings and accept their emotional reactions at face value, rather than denying the legitimacy of the feelings.

- **Communicate conjecturally, not in black or white terms.** "I am not sure what we need to do differently, but here is an idea to get our thinking going," is more effective than "You are all wrong, and here is what we need to do." One statement invites conversation, the other creates polarization–you versus them.

- **Use appeals–ask the other team members for ideas.** An opening like, "I am not sure what the best way is to increase our commitment to the decisions we make as a team. Who has an idea?" communicates a genuine willingness to explore alternatives and listen to others.

- **Neutralize emotional attachment to the issues.** Rather than denying that emotions have come into play: listen, empathize, and discuss them. A productive approach is to ask team members to consider how their emotional attachments may impact the discussion.

These approaches to communication are aimed at altering team members' perceptions of you as a superior or a threat, viewing you instead as a positive force for improving the functioning of the team. When team members feel threatened, an enormous amount of time will be spent trying to defend, be on guard, win, dominate, impress, or escape the issues—rather than considering the suggestion.

# ENCOURAGING OTHERS TO LEAD

The practices of the appointed leader will both model and set the tone for shared leadership to emerge—for many team members to have the opportunity to influence the direction or approach the team will take. The following practices will foster the leadership skills of team members and encourage them to share in leading the team:

- Communicate an expectation of involvement and participation.
- Recognize and talk about others' strengths, knowledge, expertise, and experiences.
- Be less controlling—manage by walking away.
- Acknowledge and praise any contributions from team members to the leadership role.
- Be patient. Be equally concerned with the team's effectiveness and efficiency.
- Ask questions and invite participation.

# A FINAL THOUGHT

During one teamwork session, we asked half the team to develop a list of characteristics of an effective team leader, the other half to develop a list of characteristics of effective team members. These are the two lists that were created:

### EFFECTIVE TEAM LEADERS

- Communicate
- Are open, honest, and fair
- Are consistent
- Make decisions with input
- Give subordinates the information they need to do their jobs
- Set goals and emphasize them
- Keep focused through follow-up

- Listen to feedback and ask questions
- Are loyal to the company and their subordinates
- Creates an atmosphere of growth
- Have wide visibility
- Give praise and recognition
- Constructively criticize and address problems
- Develop plans
- Have and share their mission and goals
- Are tolerant and flexible
- Are assertive
- Exhibit a willingness to change
- Treat subordinates with respect
- Are both available and accessible
- Wants to be the boss/take charge
- Has ownership for team decisions
- Sets guidelines on how to treat each other (ethics, conduct, etc.)
- Represent the team and fights a "good fight" when appropriate

## EFFECTIVE TEAM MEMBERS

- Support the leader
- Help the leader succeed
- Insure all views are explored
- Express opinions, both pro and con
- Compliment the leader on team effort
- Provide open, honest, and accurate information
- Support, protect, and defend both the team and the team leader
- Are positive and constructive
- Provide appropriate feedback
- Understand personal and team roles
- Bring problems to the team (upward feedback)
- Have ownership for team decisions
- Recognize they are a team leader

- Have a sense balance towards appropriate levels of participation
- Voluntarily participate
- Maintain confidentiality
- Are loyal to the company, their leader, and the team
- Are open to criticism and view it as an opportunity to learn
- State problems, along with alternative solutions/options
- Give praise and recognition when warranted
- Operates within the parameters of team rules

This list should dispel the notion that shared leadership results in chaos or disorganization–it is responsible maintenance of the team utilizing all the resources to their maximum. Followership in effective teams equates to being responsible for influencing the direction and processes of the team. Shared leadership is effective followership. A team that practices shared leadership, with a sensitivity to the needs of others, has fun and is a productive winner.

# APPENDIX I
# TEAM EFFECTIVENESS—
# A MODEL & QUESTIONNAIRE

If you want a way to visualize what an effective team does and to assess the strengths and weaknesses of your team against this visualization, this chapter is for you. A model of an effective team will be presented along with a questionnaire that any team can use to determine if a plan to improve teamwork is needed.

We have used both the model and questionnaire as a part of our outdoor teamwork sessions and as a stand-alone exercise that teams can use in their work environments. Teams can use this model and assessment without participating in an outdoor teamwork experience, or it can be used as subsequent follow–up assessments whenever a team wants to check on the progress that has been made since the outdoor experience.

## A MODEL OF AN EFFECTIVE TEAM

It is helpful for us and those teams we work with to have a one–page picture of areas to think about when evaluating effectiveness. The model that follows has proven to be an accurate picture of what effective teams do in five key areas:

1.  **Leadership.** The team manager uses appropriate and flexible leadership styles to develop a team approach and allocates time to improving

teamwork. Individuals other than the manager are given the opportunity to exercise leadership when their skills are appropriate to the situation facing the team. Participation and leadership are distributed among team members. The leader represents the team fairly and accurately to the rest of the organization and both monitors and influences the other four key areas in the model.

2. **Direction.** The team is clear about its values, vision, mission, strategies, goals, and priorities. These are cooperatively structured by the entire team, which results in a high degree of individual focus and commitment. The direction is felt to require stretching, but to be achievable. Energy is mainly devoted to the achievement of results.

3. **Structure/Resources.** The amount of structure and the number of procedures are viewed as appropriate by team members. Roles and responsibilities are clearly defined and differentiated among team members. Job design is changed so that the best possible match between individual goals and the team's goals can be achieved. Administrative procedures support a team approach.

4. **Atmosphere.** The team has developed an atmosphere in which people feel supported, accepted, included, trusted, and liked. Cohesion is maintained by this caring atmosphere, and feedback is both encouraged and listened to by team members. As a result, team members feel a sense of belonging and synergistic cohesiveness.

5. **Processes.** Decision-making procedures are matched to the situation. Consensus is sought for important decisions. Controversy, conflict, and differences are seen as a positive key to involvement, the quality and creativity of decisions, and the continuance of the group in good working condition. Communication is two-way, with emphasis on the accurate expression of both ideas and feelings. Ability and information determine the influence of team members. The members periodically evaluate the effectiveness of the team and decide how to improve its functioning.

# TEAM EFFECTIVENESS MODEL

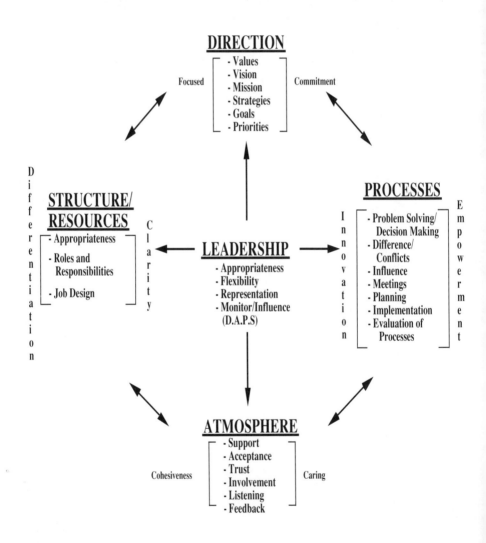

# TEAM EFFECTIVENESS QUESTIONNAIRE

Fifty statements are listed below. Think about each statement in relation to your work team. Use the Team Effectiveness Answer Grid to respond to the statements. If you feel that a statement is basically true, mark a **T** by the appropriate number on the answer grid. If you feel that a statement is false, mark an **F** by the appropriate number on the answer grid.

Remember that the quality of the results is directly related to your own openness when answering the questions. This is not meant to be a scientific survey, but rather a tool to provoke thought and discussion. Work methodically through all fifty questions and reach a decision either to put a **T** or **F** by the appropriate number on the answer grid.

When you see the following term(s), please keep these definitions in mind:

**VISION:** A description of the desired state, values, credos, or guiding principles for the team which includes but is not limited to how the team should treat the users of their service and each other.

**MISSIONS:** The specific task or business the team is charged with and the desired quality of its outputs.

**GOALS:** Individual and group-specific priorities for a given time period, usually a year.

**STRATEGIES:** A planned course of action and allocation of resources necessary for movement toward goals and the mission.

1. The values and goals of the group are not a satisfactory integration and expression of the relevant values and needs of the members.

2. The team leader is hard to influence.

3. All the interactions and problem-solving and decision-making activities of the group occur in a non-supportive atmosphere.

4. There often is confusion about assignments or unclear relationships between people on this team.

5. Differences or conflicts are denied, suppressed, or avoided at all costs.

6. Each member of my work group does not have a very clear idea of the group's vision.

7. The team manager is uncomfortable sharing leadership and decision making in a participative atmosphere.

8. People only pay attention to some team members and not to others.

9. There is often confusion in the team over who is responsible for what.

10. My work group often acts without planning enough.

11. There is a low commitment to our vision and goals.

12. The team manager does not adapt his/her style to changing circumstances.

13. People do not seem concerned with helping each other get the job done; everyone is pulling in opposite directions or out for themselves.

14. Different people on the job are always asking me to do different things at the same time; as a result I feel I have to juggle too many balls at once.

15. After the team sits down to discuss something, I usually walk away wondering what we just did and what is supposed to happen next.

16. The task or objectives of the group are not well understood or accepted by the members.

17. People are not encouraged to work together towards a better team effort.

18. There is a lack of innovation, risk taking, imagination, or taking initiative in this team.

19. The team's manager and members spend little time in clarifying what they expect and need from one another.

20. Important issues often are "swept under the carpet" and not worked through.

21. Some team members are not really committed to the success of the team.

22. The team manager is not sufficiently sensitive to the different needs of each member.

23. Poor communications are evident in this team: people are afraid to speak up; we do not listen to each other or talk together.

24. The objectives of some individual team members do not gel with those of other members.

25. Attempts to review events critically are seen as negative and harmful.

26. There is no regular review of individual objectives and priorities.

27. The team manager gets little information about how the team sees his/her performance.

28. There is a lack of trust between manager and members or between the members of this team.

29. Team members are uncertain about their individual roles in relation to the team.

30. We function in a rather rigid manner and are not sufficiently flexible in using team resources.

31. We do not have an adequate way to establish our team's vision, objectives, and strategies.

32. The team leader does not represent the team adequately to the rest of the organization.

33. There are cliques and political maneuvering in the team.

34. The team does not have adequate administrative resources and procedures.

35. Little time is spent on reviewing what the team does, how it works, and how to improve it.

36. We do not work within clear strategic guidelines.

37. The team leader does not monitor or help us review our direction, team structure, or ability to work as a team.

38. Members often restrain their critical remarks to avoid "rocking the boat."

39. I often feel my job is not very satisfying or significant in its contribution to the team's efforts.

40. We often fail to finish things satisfactorily.

41. The objectives of our team are not really understood by everyone.

42. Team members are often unwilling to take the initiative for unassigned tasks.

43. A person would be a fool to be himself/herself in this team.

44. Members of this team seldom use one another as a resource.

45. The team is not good at learning from its mistakes.

46. The team's objectives have not been systematically related to the objectives of the whole organization.

47. As long as performance is satisfactory, the leader is not particularly concerned about the degree of teamwork displayed.

48. In group discussion, team members often hide their real motives.

49. We would be more effective as a unit if we were organized differently.

50. Creative ideas often are not followed through to definite actions.

# TEAM EFFECTIVENESS ANSWER GRID

- In The grid shown here, there are 50 squares. Each one numbered to correspond to the statements on the questionnaire.
- If you think a statement is basically true about your team, mark a **T** in the square. If you feel a statement is false, mark an **F** in the appropriate square.
- Fill in the top line first, working from left to right; then fill in the second line, etc.
- When you have responded to all 50 statements, total the number of **T**'s in each of the vertical columns, and write the total in the space shown at the bottom of the column.

| 1 | 2 | 3 | 4 | 5 |
|---|---|---|---|---|
| 6 | 7 | 8 | 9 | 10 |
| 11 | 12 | 13 | 14 | 15 |
| 16 | 17 | 18 | 19 | 20 |
| 21 | 22 | 23 | 24 | 25 |
| 26 | 27 | 28 | 29 | 30 |
| 31 | 32 | 33 | 34 | 35 |
| 36 | 37 | 38 | 39 | 40 |
| 41 | 42 | 43 | 44 | 45 |
| 46 | 47 | 48 | 49 | 50 |

Total Number of T's

| I | II | III | IV | V |

# TEAM EFFECTIVENESS INTERPETATION SHEET

When you have totaled all the **T**'s in each of the five vertical columns of the Answer Grid, copy these totals for each team member next to the appropriate Roman numerals on the chart shown here:

| TEAM MEMBER | 1 | 2 | 3 | 4 | 5 | 6 | 7 | 8 | 9 | 10 | TEAM TOTAL | TEAM RANKING |
|---|---|---|---|---|---|---|---|---|---|---|---|---|
| I. DIRECTION | | | | | | | | | | | | |
| II. LEADERSHIP | | | | | | | | | | | | |
| III. ATMOSPHERE | | | | | | | | | | | | |
| IV. STRUCTURE/ RESOURCES | | | | | | | | | | | | |
| V. PROCESSES | | | | | | | | | | | | |

Next, add the individual team members totals for each of the five rows and place these in the box titled TEAM TOTAL. Lastly, in the TEAM RANKING BOX, assign each of the five rows a number from 1 for the highest TEAM TOTAL to 5 for the lowest TEAM TOTAL.

Allow each team member to comment on his/her agreement with the TEAM RANKING of the relative strengths (numerical ranking 4 and 5) and weaknesses (numerical ranking 1 and 2) for this team.

# APPENDIX II
# USING OUTDOOR ADVENTURE-BASED TRAINING TO EMPOWER YOUR TEAM

The media have presented adventure-based training as full of thrills and chills–"going for it," wild, or macho endeavors similar to boot-camp experiences. If this is what you are seeking for your team, take them on vacation to some exotic, out-of-the-way place.

In contrast to this view, if you are considering using outdoor adventure-based training to improve teamwork, we suggest that you consider a few basic questions before making a decision.

## WHY DOES THE TRAINING HAVE TO BE EXPERIENTIAL?

Working with many teams has led us to conclude that we cannot teach anything to anyone. In helping each team to better understand itself, the team's members are the only resource available. To understand relationships among team members or emotions that impact teamwork, the individuals are the only experience the team has. The facts and answers concerning teamwork are revealed only when team members have the courage to face a wide range of situations with as many teammates as possible.

133

For the training to have both high impact and lasting effect, it must be experiential and not didactic. By placing all our bets on experience, we express our conviction that it will reveal a team's and individual member's behavior so that team members can examine it, openly discuss it, and learn from it. The trick is to apply the awareness gained from the experience to real-world situations. Experiential exercises create an environment in which to establish the foundation upon which the steps necessary in application can be built.

Team growth has a price: discomfort. In adventure-based programs, discomfort has also been called "challenge," or "stretching the limit," to soften the price a team must pay for peak performance. For some teams the discomfort hinges on success or failure, on not being perfect, letting go of control, or allowing their thoughts and feelings to flow freely.

The reality is that each team and its individual members will have to experience their own discomforts to find their answers for peak performance. They can't read the solutions in a book or find them in a lecture or on a audio tape.

## WHY GO OUTDOORS?

The outdoors is a beautiful classroom that teaches through natural rather than contrived consequences. We have yet to find another medium with as dramatic an impact. Individual behavior is inescapable, and it is punished or rewarded with unbelievable neutrality. If an individual doesn't listen to the ideas of other group members on how to move the team across a river and his idea fails, the team gets wet. Everyone gets wet, regardless of sex, brains, color, or religion.

Outdoor experiences encourage people to behave as they would in the real world, where their egos and personal needs are on the line.

In the outdoors every conceivable human condition, emotion, problem, and excuse are possible.

All the events presented here can be conducted indoors–they work. Being outdoors adds richness, excitement, and credibility to the metaphor. You don't have to go to exotic places–state and national parks close to your location work fine. A lack of commitment, not budgetary constraints, should be the only factor keeping you from going outdoors. Our caution: doing an event indoors for two hours is a training simulation, not an extended live-in intervention to coax out and facilitate improvements in issues impeding teamwork.

O.K., so you think adventure-based experiential training would help your team or clients. Before you charge off to the woods, sea, or mountains, you need to give some attention to five additional questions:

## 1. HOW SHOULD THE EXERCISES BE SEQUENCED?

For us, team growth and improvement constitute a cyclical process that begins with the recognition and acceptance of nonproductive behaviors. The phases that complete the process are:

Self-managing teams periodically recycle through this process. Events are ordered in light of this cyclical process, with the addition of an orientation event:

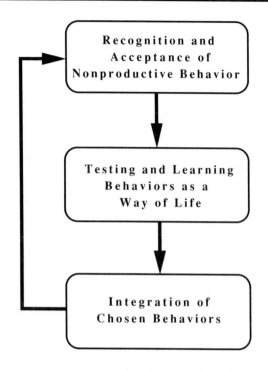

| Event | Purpose |
|-------|---------|

- Orientation
  - Explore the nature of experiential learning
  - Clarify the facilitator's role
  - Establish the expectations of participants
  - Clarify the roles of team members and leader

- Confrontation
  - Develop undeniable data on the internal issues fostering and impeding teamwork

| | | |
|---|---|---|
| • Testing and Learning | - | Provide the opportunity for team members to experiment with new behaviors |
| | - | Test the usefulness of different ways of behaving as means to improve overall team effectiveness |
| | - | Define specific actions that can be implemented for improved team effectiveness |
| • Successful Application | - | Discover the benefits of the newly defined team and bonding behaviors |
| | - | Experience some success |
| | - | Develop team cohesiveness and a belief that team members can operate effectively |
| | - | Establish a "we can do it" attitude |

Regardless of program length, the objective is to enable the team to come face to face with undeniable evidence of their behavior, to experiment with new behavior, and to end in a whole state. A teamwork session should never end without the opportunity for the team to successfully apply what they have learned and to feel good about themselves.

## 2.   WHAT ARE THE OBJECTIVES OF AN ADVENTURE-BASED EXERCISE?

One school of thought holds that what teams and individuals learn from an exercise cannot be pre-defined; each will take away something unique. We believe this is an excuse for inadequate attention to the objectives the team wants to achieve, problems in how the exercise is structured, and unfocused facilitation after the event. Each exercise can be designed to produce predictable outcomes.

From reading the narratives in this book, you may feel that the objective, regardless of the exercise, is for the team to fail. In fact, the exercises are designed for the group to be challenged but to have some hope of accomplishment. Failure contributes to team growth only if the team believes it can accomplish the exercise. An exercise that has less than a 50% chance of success should be questioned.

Without direction for each exercise, the experience may provide an exciting day with only minimal learning. The objective for the event gives it a direction and purpose; it must rely directly upon some human capacity. To build trust among team members is not an objective until specific human behaviors are defined:

- To relinquish control and be vulnerable
- To give up assumptions and take risks
- To select a support person
- To ask for help
- To learn to depend on others
- To value differences among team members
- To share leadership

In response to this definition, an objective might read:

To increase the capacity of team members to value their differences by having each participant understand the needs of fellow

team members as he/she participates in a
cave rescue scenario.

Or

To increase the capacity of individuals to
share leadership by rotating this role during
an orienteering scenario.

Many topics of discussion may come from the cave or orienteering
scenarios, and that is fine, but the facilitator has a clear sense of
direction and focus. The activity will create the learning, and the
team members will begin the process of accepting trust as part of
this team's norms.

## 3.   HOW WILL THE EXERCISE BE STRUCTURED?

Setting up or structuring an activity is tightly linked to the creative
art of facilitation. The exercise is designed so that the key issues
surrounding the objective are brought to the surface. These
include which team member performs which task, what special
conditions are placed upon the team and team members, the order
of participation, pairing of team members, time limits, and, in fact,
any aspect that does not jeopardize team safety.

Structuring an exercise is not a random procedure based upon the
needs of the facilitator but one determined by the exercise's
objective. The desired outcome is to increase the intensity of the
activity and bring issues surrounding the objective to the
surface–not to build in more difficulty or to induce failure.

Structuring of the exercise is not designed for show or to create a
power struggle between the facilitator and team; the intent is to
make evident the behavior of the team and thus achieve the
objective of the exercise. Muting all the male members of a team

and placing the female members in the lead can spotlight sex-role stereotypes or illustrate how the team accepts differences in members' abilities, motives, and skills.

## 4.     HOW WILL THE EXERCISE BE PROCESSED?

In discussing the issues that were revealed in the exercise team members experience the real discomfort and growth. Issues are the various thoughts, perceptions, feelings, and actions of team members during an exercise.

In developing the objective, structuring the experience, and facilitating the discussion, the challenge for the facilitator is to force the issues out of hiding and then use experiential evidence in the form of concrete examples that illustrate the team's behavior. In many cases, team members may be too eager to deny or attempt to rationalize this evidence away.

All structuring of an exercise is aimed at exposing key issues by providing a team with evidence of its own behavior. For example, if the team is really two competitive groups, structuring a cave-rescue exercise so that one group is given the opportunity to cooperate or compete with the other group vividly exposes a key issue for that team. Based on the group's choice, the evidence is out in the open for all to examine and discuss.

The importance of the experience in exposing issues that accurately reflect a team's behavior cannot be overemphasized. For individual or team growth, key issues must surface and be experientially challenged. No team member is going to work on an issue without proof that his or her perception is wrong, and all the dialogue in the world will not provide this proof. Facilitators must be sensitive enough to understand the major issues for the team, allow the experience to provide the proof, and then keep the group's discussion focused on the issue(s).

## 5. DOES MY TEAM NEED A FACILITATOR?

It is impossible for us to be objective on this point. Recognizing that our view may be biased, we believe that the initial outdoor exercises aimed at improving teamwork require facilitation.

A facilitator's client is the individuals who compose the team. He or she must understand what they want to accomplish and have a good picture of the team's strengths, weaknesses, and important issues. The facilitator must then structure the exercises to achieve the client's objectives, provide cognitive input or models for a common way of analyzing and discussing issues, and direct the discussion so that the issues are confronted and the actions are defined.

A facilitator is the conduit for the group, helping them discuss uncomfortable issues. The facilitator's responsibility is to push the group in the face of his/her own discomfort and the possibility of emotional responses from team members. If other team members attempt to rescue a person or defuse the discussion, the facilitator's role is to persist and turn the issue right back to the team or member for solution. Without this gentle guidance and prodding, little team growth occurs.

We strongly believe in the need for a facilitator, but advise that the selection be made with great care. Using the outdoors for improved teamwork is not a mechanical process. Safety is of paramount importance, but once these mechanics are satisfied, the orchestrating and processing of events are more an art form than a science. Facilitation requires experience in knowing how far to push a group; in fighting their egos; in being human, caring, and accepting of the process of facilitating as a means to grow; and in being clear on where the individual facilitator is in his/her own life. Not everyone can be a facilitator. Nor can all outdoor technicians facilitate a team.

Our ideal is for an internal and an external facilitator to work with the team. The external is not bound by politics and is freer to push the leader and the team. The internal person brings the experience of working with other teams in the same company and the realities of the given company to the discussion.

# A FINAL THOUGHT

Working with a team in the outdoors should be viewed as the first step towards growth in team effectiveness, not as the end. Events like those described in this book lay the foundation for increased trust, bonding, openness, and support among team members.

Effective teams will use this foundation as a starting point for planned periodic discussions as to how well the team is functioning and for problem solving in areas where improvements are needed. These discussions will give equal time to examining both *what* the team does and *how* the members operate as a group. The *how* discussions will benefit the most from the common outdoor experience; their success will depend on the ability of team members to be open, honest, trusting, and supportive of one another.

The outdoor experience is not a cure-all but a therapeutic foundation that the team can use back at work to build a healthy and more effective team. To achieve this will require the manager and team continually to be sensitive to and willing to discuss the issues that are barriers for the team. As a result of the outdoor experience, the team will never be the same. Our goal is for team managers or group facilitators to use this experience to enhance the team's effectiveness and build on the experience back to the work place.

Just a pleasant memory, or a foundation for future team growth and strength? The choice is yours!

# Apendix III
# Facilitating Team
# Building Outdoors

Much has been written on the impact of a facilitator's style on the learning process of a particular team. Although facilitation style–tone, silence, constructive confrontation, the use of behavioral notes, etc.–is a critical issue for you to resolve, it is not the focus of this appendix. Rather, we look here at the unique challenges facing the facilitator working outdoors.

## WHAT IS THE REAL EVENT?

When a team is in residence outdoors, the opportunity arises for functional or dysfunctional member behavior to occur at any point during the day. Some of the most significant learning takes place as a result of behavior on the way to, in preparation for, or after an event. If you focus only on what happens during a scheduled activity, you may miss the "real event" that is unfolding.

For example, one team had to walk two miles to the location where the activity was to occur. The trip required the team to traverse a significant climb in elevation through thick brush. The leaders, oblivious to the needs of other team members, set a grilling pace, even though no time constraints were placed on the journey. One member was in poorer condition than the others and, as a result, lagged behind; his ability to complete the journey was at times in doubt. Two other members were wearing walking shorts and received many scratches as they tried to keep pace with the leaders. Their repeated pleas for a slower, more cautious journey were ignored.

A facilitator could choose either to intervene and ask the leaders to slow down the pace or to let the "real event" unfold. Taking the latter approach created an opportunity for a rich discussion focused on these issues: What is the level of sensitivity of team members to the needs of others and the differences in their ability or capability? Who sets the pace for the team, and what happens when others can't meet this expectations? What responsibility do team members accept for helping others? Do team members feel comfortable asking for assistance, are they heard, and what does this say about the level of support and cooperation within the team? In this case the members' behavior during the journey was the "real event"—it was alive with data for group discussion and problem solving.

# WHAT, SO WHAT, NOW WHAT?

Discussing just the activity focuses on **WHAT** happened: who did what, when, where, and how? At least three levels can be pursued in this discussion:

- The behavior exhibited during the activity
- The feelings generated by this behavior
- The core issues underlying the behavior

Each successive level moves farther away from the actual event and is more difficult and potentially more disquieting. In our opinion, the biggest failure in using experiential learning is to focus just on the behavior exhibited during the activity. Courage on the part of the facilitator is needed to leave the event and start to question or make hypotheses with the group about the effects this behavior may have on team member feelings and/or operations of the team. The team will struggle to focus only on the tangible behavior that occurred during the event–it is safe. The fruitful discussion concerns not the activity itself–this team will never face this event on the job—but the underlying issues and the effect they have on each team member.

The content of each activity is to serve as a metaphor for how the team functions in the real world. Pushing the team beyond a simple discussion of the activity into the similarities that exist between the behavior exhibited and how the team solves problems, the inclusion or exclusion of team members, how decisions are made, what roles members assume in team projects, communication patterns, etc., moves the discussion into the **SO WHAT** area.

The real payoff is for team members to reach agreement on how they can apply what they have learned to real world situations— **NOW WHAT**. Unfortunately, many discussions go no deeper than a simple review of the activity. The key is to guide the discussion away from the event and to see it as a metaphor. Decisions regarding office applications can be then generated. A simple rule of thumb is to spend 20% of the discussion time on **WHAT** and 80% on **SO WHAT** and **NOW WHAT**.

## OUTPUT VS. EVENT FOCUS

The events are a means to an end–improved teamwork through better cooperation, communication, support, use of resources, better group processes, clearer direction or changes in the style of leadership. The facilitator must be clear on the ends and then orchestrate the events to maximize the likelihood of these ends being achieved. In too many cases, adventure-based training focus only on events–the days are filled with activities, with little thought as to their sequence, relevance, or interrelationship.

All facilitators need an effective teamwork paradigm to guide them in thinking through the total design, in not just throwing together a group of activities. As our guide, we use the model discussed in Appendix I. Four questions are key to the design: Why are you asking the team to do this? What aspect of effective teamwork needs to be highlighted? What is the team likely to learn, and how can team members apply this insight to the type of work they do in the real world?

# INDIVIDUAL VS. TEAM FOCUS

We believe that the successful completion of an outdoor activity should require team effort and problem solving. Events that focus on individuals are focused events–high ropes, rappeling, rock climbing, zip line, pamper pole, and tyrolian traverse–are useful to develop personal insight, courage, and risk taking, but they are out of place when the focus is on the team. We encourage you to be creative in developing team-focused activities. The added benefit of not using individual focused events is that you don't have to be concerned with safety riggings or tied into one location. Team-focused events can be done anywhere.

# FLEXIBLE VS. RIGID

As a facilitator you have to be flexible–ready to abort your plans and to spend time with the team on the issues that are most pressing for them. After observing a team in action, the facilitator will often spend time identifying and problem solving the team's weaknesses and building on their strengths, rather than moving forward to a new activity.

This discussion could include defining what type of team they want to strive towards; helping them clarify the team's strategy, mission, and/or objectives; confronting substandard individual performance; and establishing contracts between team members as to what they want, more or less of, from other individuals on the team. A sensitivity to the real issues that face each team and then flexibility to continue with not just the outdoor exercises but to structure the time to discuss and solve problems is required. Locking into a schedule will result in both team member and facilitator frustration.

## WHAT WILL YOU LEAVE THEM?

Your objective is to leave the team with a tangible plan that will allow them to become self-managing. Simply mimicking the facilitator is not learning. Team members need to understand the process they are going through and develop a comfortable way of operating so they can carry on by themselves after you depart.

We have found it useful to present simplified processes that they can adapt to their own situations. Some of these process are how to define leadership and team member expectations; how to manage conflict and differences; how to define which decisions require total team participation, no participation, or just discussion; how to monitor the team's internal climate; how to manage the consensus process; and how to conduct their team meeting more effectively. Our goal is to provide teams with tools in a simple format that can be remembered and used–if the process can't be covered on one page, it needs to be simplified.

Just leaving the team with memories of the activities is not fulfilling your role as a facilitator. You need to empower them to function on their own.

Although not all inclusive, thinking through these unique challenges before you start the outdoor training will increase you chances of being a supportive, helpful change agent with the teams you facilitate.